A

GRAMMAR

OF THE

MASSACHUSETTS INDIAN LANGUAGE.

BY JOHN ELIOT.

———

A NEW EDITION:

WITH NOTES AND OBSERVATIONS,

BY

PETER S. DU PONCEAU, LL. D.

AND

AN INTRODUCTION AND SUPPLEMENTARY
OBSERVATIONS,

BY

JOHN PICKERING.

———

AS PUBLISHED IN THE MASSACHUSETTS HISTORICAL COLLECTIONS.

———

BOSTON:

PRINTED BY PHELPS AND FARNHAM.

1822.

MASSACHUSETTS LANGUAGE.

INTRODUCTORY OBSERVATIONS.

THE languages of the American Indians, however little value may be attached to them, as the source of what is frequently (though without much discrimination) called useful knowledge, have for some time deeply engaged the attention of the learned in Europe, as exhibiting numerous phenomena, if the term may be applied, the knowledge of which will be found indispensable to a just theory of speech. It is true, indeed, that we have long had our systems of *universal grammar*, or in other words our theories of language, as deduced from the small number of European and Oriental tongues, which have been the subject of investigation with scholars; just as in the physical sciences we have had, for example, our theories of chemistry, founded upon the comparatively small number of phenomena, which had been observed in past ages. But the discovery of numerous facts of the most surprising character in that science, even within our own memory, has compelled the chemists of the present age to re-examine the old, and resort to new theories; and from the great advances made in *Comparative Philology* in the present age, particularly by means of an extensive acquaintance with the *unwritten* dialects of barbarous nations, there is reason to believe that some important modifications are yet to be made in our theories of language.

Among the unwritten languages, those of the continent of America present us with many new and striking facts. If we may adopt the opinions of a learned Society in another part of our country, there appears to be "a wonderful organization, which distinguishes the languages of the Aborigines of this country from all other idioms of the known world;" and they shew us "how little the world has yet advanced in that science which is proudly called

Universal Grammar."* We find in them (according to a learned member of the same Society) "a *new* manner of compounding words from various roots, so as to strike the mind at once with a whole mass of ideas ; a new manner of expressing the cases of substantives by inflecting the verbs which govern them : a new number (the *particular plural*) applied to the declension of nouns and conjugations of verbs ; a new concordance in tense of the conjunction with the verb ; we see not only pronouns, as in the Hebrew and some other languages, but adjectives, conjunctions, adverbs, combined with the principal part of speech, and producing an immense variety of verbal forms ;" it is also one of the most remarkable characteristicks of the American languages, that they are " entirely deficient of our auxiliary verbs *to have* and *to be :*" " There are no words that I know of (says the same distinguished philologist) in any American idioms to express abstractedly the ideas signified by those two verbs."†

Some of the facts here stated, however extraordinary they may be thought by speculative persons, who have formed their theories upon the study of the European languages alone, will be found to have been noticed in the following Grammar of the venerable *Eliot*, composed at the distance of a century and a half from our own age, and long before any favourite theory or philological enthusiasm can be supposed to have warped the judgment of the writer and led him to distort his facts, in order to make them suit an ingenious hypothesis. The editor cannot refrain from selecting two or three instances, in which this indefatigable man, from an examination of a very limited number of kindred dialects in this part of the continent, has given similar views to those, which are more fully presented by the learned writer just cited ; who has extended his investigations to numerous dialects from the northern to the southern extremity of America.

Of the general power of *compounding* words, for example, *Eliot* (without however describing the particular

* Transactions of the Historical and Literary Committee of the American Philosophical Society at Philadelphia, vol. i. p. xii.

† *Ibid.* Report of Mr. Du Ponceau on the Indian Languages, p. xxxviii. xl.

mode) says—" This language doth greatly delight in *compounding of words*, for abbreviation, to speak much in few words, though they be sometimes long ; which is chiefly caused by the many syllables which the Grammar Rule requires, and *suppletive* syllables, which are of no signification, and curious care of Euphonie."* On the subject of the *declensions* he observes—" The variation of Nouns is not by *male* and *female*, as in other, learned languages, and in European nations they do . . . . . There be two forms or declensions of Nouns, *animate, inanimate.* 1. The *animate* form or declension is, when the thing signified is a living creature ; and such Nouns do always make their plural in *og*, as wosketomp, *man*, wosketompaog ; *a* is but for euphonie. 2. The *inanimate* form or declension of Nouns is, when the thing signified is not a living creature ; and these make the plural in *ash ;* as hussun, *a stone*, hussunash."† Again—in respect to that extraordinary characteristick of the Indian languages, the want of the *substantive verb*, Eliot says—" We have no compleat distinct word for the *Verb Substantive*, as the learned languages and our English Tongue have, but it is under a regular composition, whereby *many words* are made Verb Substantive." Of this mode of forming verbs he then gives the following among other examples : " The first sort of Verb Substantives is made by adding any of these terminations to the word ; yeuꝏ, aꝏ, oꝏ, with due euphonie ; and this is so, be the word a noun, as woske-

---

* Indian Gram. p. 6.

† *Ibid.* p. 8, 9, 10. The Rev. Mr. Heckewelder, in his interesting Correspondence with Mr. Du Ponceau, gives the same account of the *Delaware* language of the present day : " In the Indian languages (says he) those discriminating words or inflections, which we call *genders*, are not, as with us, in general intended to distinguish between *male* and *female* beings, but between *animate* and *inanimate* things or substances." He adds that " *trees* and *plants* (annual plants and grasses excepted) are included within the generick class of *animated* beings." On this latter point, however, Eliot says, that *all* Vegetables are of the *inanimate* form ; and he then gives these two examples ; " *mehtug*, a tree, *mehtugquash ; moskeht*, grass, *moskehtuash.*" Whether this difference of opinion arises from a difference between the two dialects in this particular, or from some other cause, the editor has not yet been able to ascertain.

2

tompoœ, *he is a man ;* or *adnoun*, as wompiyeuœ, *it is white ;* or be the word an *adverb*, or the like."*

It is unnecessary to enumerate further particulars in respect to the languages of our own part of the country. It should not, however, be overlooked, that the same observations which Eliot and others have made respecting the *northern* dialects, appear to be generally applicable to those of the *south* and other parts of the continent. The editor is the more strongly impelled to extend his remarks on this point, because the plausible opinions, or rather amusing dreams, of certain philosophers (as they are sometimes styled) have still an influence among us, and continue to give currency to speculative errours instead of established facts.

Of these erroneous opinions, founded upon very limited inquiries into the languages of the globe, an ample specimen is given by *Clavigero*, in his valuable *History of Mexico ;* where they are also most thoroughly refuted by an appeal to *facts.* To this intelligent author, indeed, subsequent writers, both in our own country and in Europe, have been much indebted, not only for the correction of errours which had been successfully propagated respecting these languages, but also for a refutation of the unfounded opinions of eminent naturalists and philosophers respecting the degeneracy of the animal and other productions of this continent. It will not be useless or out of place, so far as respects the *languages* of America, to advert briefly to those opinions ; because they still have, as above observed, an influence in perpetuating errour.

In respect to the *general character* of these languages, (to adopt the remarks of Mr. Du Ponceau) " it has been

---

* Indian Gram. p. 15. This want of the verb *to be* is also noticed in *Edwards's* valuable *Observations on the Language of the Muhhekaneew* [Mohegan] *Indians*, published at New Haven in the year 1788. " They have (says Edwards) no verb substantive in all the language. Therefore they cannot say, *he is a man, he is a coward,* &c. They express the same by one word, which is a verb neuter, viz. *nemannauwoo*, he is a man. *Nemannauw* is the noun substantive *man :* that turned into a verb neuter of the third person singular becomes *nemannauwoo*, as in Latin it is said *Græcor, Græcatur,* &c. Thus they turn any substantive whatever into a verb neuter." The learned author adds in a note—" The circumstance that they have no verb substantive, accounts for their not using that verb, when they speak English. They say, *I man, I sick,*" &c. p. 14.

said and will be said again, that savages, having but few ideas, can want but few words, and therefore that their languages must necessarily be poor." To which the same learned writer thus answers by a direct appeal to the simple fact : " Whether savages have or have not many ideas, it is not my province to determine ; all I can say is, that if it is true that their ideas are few, it is not less certain that they have many words to express them." He then concludes his remarks in these strong terms : " For my own part, I confess that I am lost in astonishment at the *copiousness* and admirable structure of their languages ; for which I can only account by looking up to the GREAT FIRST CAUSE."*

To the same effect are the observations of the venerable Mr. Heckewelder, whose fidelity, and intelligence, and skill (in the Delaware dialect in particular) are beyond all question. In one of his letters he tells Mr. Du Ponceau, that he must not " imagine that their languages are poor" —that he will be still more pleased as he becomes more familiar " with the *beautiful* idiom of the Lenni Lennape" —" I should never have done, (he adds) were I to endeavour to explain to you in all their details the various modes which the Indians have of expressing their ideas, shades of ideas and combinations of ideas," &c.†

Will any one require a confirmation of the testimony of persons circumstanced as these two writers are ; the one distinguished for those habits of accurate investigation which belong to his profession, and the other for that perfect and minute knowledge of his subject, which is the natural result of forty years' study ? If such confirmation should be required, it will be found at large, in the work of Clavigero above cited, where the author refutes in detail many erroneous opinions respecting America, which had so long prevailed. He thus quotes a celebrated writer on this subject : " The languages of America are so limited and so scarce of words, that it is impossible to express any *metaphysical* idea in them. In no one of those languages

* Report of Mr. Du Ponceau, p. xxvii—xxix.
† Correspondence, p. 368, 377, 393.

can they count above the number *three.* It is impossible to translate a book either into the languages of the Algonquines or Paraguese, or even into those of Mexico or Peru, on account of their not having sufficient plenty of proper terms to express general ideas." To which Clavigero replies : " We have (says he) learned the Mexican, and have heard it spoken by the Mexicans for many years, but never knew that it was deficient in numerical terms, and words signifying universal ideas," &c. " *We know* that the Mexicans had numeral words to express as many thousands or millions as they pleased ;" and the author then subjoins a long list of them, extending to very high numbers. He then shows that the writers whom he is here opposing, are equally wrong in asserting that these languages cannot express *metaphysical* ideas ; and he affirms " that it is not easy to find a language more fit to treat on metaphysical subjects than the Mexican, as it would be difficult to find another which abounds so much in abstract terms," equivalents to many of which, he declares, cannot be found " in the Hebrew, in the Greek, in the Latin, in the French, in the Italian, in the English, in the Spanish or Portuguese ;" and he gives his readers a list of abstract terms with the corresponding Mexican words, " which (he observes) are understood by the rudest Indians." He adds, that it is by means of this abundance of words of this kind, that the deepest mysteries of religion have been explained in that language, and that various books of the Scriptures, and the works of Thomas à Kempis and others, have been translated into it ; which, as he justly remarks, could not have been done if the language had been deficient in terms of this nature. The same observations, he says, are applicable to all the languages spoken in the dominions of Mexico, as Grammars and Dictionaries and treatises on religion have been published in them, as well as in the Mexican.*

Such, then, is the character of the languages spoken by the inhabitants of the *middle* region of this continent ; and since the publication of Clavigero's work, we have

* Clavigero's Mexico, *Dissertat.* vi. *Sect.* 6 ; in vol. 2, edit. 1787.

been enabled to obtain authentick information of various other languages; particularly of one of the most southern, that of *Chili*, (or the Araucanian, as it is often called,) an account of which is given in the Abbé *Molina's* excellent History of Chili. It will, assuredly, surprise most readers to find how exactly the account given of this language by Molina (who furnishes us with facts instead of hypotheses) corresponds with what Clavigero says of the Mexican; and how completely at variance they both are with those of the speculative writers above alluded to. "So *copious* is the *Chilian* language (says the author) that, in the opinion of those well acquainted with it, a complete dictionary thereof would require more than one large volume; for, besides the radical words, which are very numerous, so great is the use of *compounds*, that it may almost be said in this consists the very genius of the language." Again—"*Abstract* nouns are very frequent;" and, in another place he states, as a remarkable property of this language, that it makes "frequent use of abstract nouns in a peculiar manner. Thus, instead of saying *pu Huinca*, the Spaniards, they commonly say, *Huincagen*, the Spaniolity; *tamén cuiàgen*, your trio, that is, you other three; *épu tamen cajugen layai*, two of you other six will die—*literally*, two of your sixths." The author also mentions in this language (as Eliot, Edwards and others do in the case of the northern dialects) the "practice of converting all the parts of speech into verbs, in such a manner that the whole knowledge of the Chilian language may be said to consist in the management of the verbs."* He adds, that "*proper names* are also susceptible of this elegance. Thus from *Pedro*, is formed the verb *Petron*, to be Pedro; *Petrobui*, was Pedro . . . . Owing to this property, the translation of European works into the Chilian is very easy, in which, instead of losing any of their spirit and elegance, they acquire a degree of precision even superiour to the originals. This, among other instances that

---

* To the same effect, Eliot says of the *Massachusetts* language—"The manner of *formation* of the nouns and verbs have such a latitude of use, that *there needeth little other Syntaxis in the language.*"—Indian Gram. p. 23.

might be mentioned, is strongly evinced in the *Christian Thoughts* of the celebrated Bouhours, which was translated in the year 1713.   There can be no better test of a language than its *translations*, as its comparative richness or poverty is rendered more apparent in this mode than in any other."*

But it may possibly still be urged, that whatever is the fact with respect to the languages of Mexico, Chili, and the more civilized parts of the continent, yet the dialects of the more barbarous nations must be extremely poor and deficient in the particulars above considered. As to some of these very dialects, however, we have the unequivocal testimony of Mr. Heckewelder and Mr. Du Ponceau already cited ; and their opinion is supported by that of writers who have preceded them.   It may, perhaps, appear somewhat like want of respect to persons so well known as those gentlemen are, to adduce the testimony of others in support of their statements ; but such has been the influence of the opposite opinion on this subject, that the editor trusts he shall be pardoned for briefly recurring to two or three preceding writers ; whose observations in this instance are the more important, as they are founded upon the dialects of the *northern* nations alone.   *Colden* informs us, that " the Six Nations compound their words without end, whereby their language becomes sufficiently copious."   *Edwards* observes —" It has been said, that savages have no parts of speech beside the substantive and the verb.   This is not true concerning the *Mohegan*, nor concerning any other tribe of Indians of whose languages I have any knowledge. The Mohegans have all the eight parts of speech to be found in other languages."   Again—" It has been said also, that savages never abstract, and have no abstract terms ; which with regard to the Mohegans is another mistake.....I doubt not, but that there is in this language the full proportion of abstract to concrete terms, which is commonly to be found in other languages."†   The late

* *Molina's Hist. of Chili*, vol. ii. p. 5, 297, 303, 301, *American translation*.
† *Observations*, &c. p. 10.

Mr. Zeisberger affirmed the Iroquois language (in which he was thoroughly skilled) to be very copious. Roger Williams, who was distinguished for his skill in the Indian languages, in speaking of the dialect of the Naragansets, declares in emphatick terms, that "their language is exceeding copious, and they have five or six words sometimes for one thing."* If any further proof were necessary in this case, we have it conclusively in the single fact, that *Eliot* found a sufficient stock of words in the *Massachusetts* dialect, for *a complete translation of the Old and New Testaments.*

Such, then, are some of the striking facts, which the investigation of these remarkable dialects has already brought into view; and facts of this novel character could not fail to stimulate the curiosity of all, who take an interest in the study of man, particularly of his distinguishing characteristick, the faculty of speech. For, if there is any utility in studying language philosophically, (which all admit,) then it is manifestly indispensable for those, who claim the rank of philosophical grammarians, to make themselves in some degree acquainted with the languages of the barbarous, as well as of the civilized nations of the globe. Accordingly, the illustrious scholars of Europe, particularly of Germany, have for some time past, with their well known ardour and perseverance, been pursuing their researches into the curious dialects of this continent; and they have already examined, with no inconsiderable degree of minuteness, such a number of them as will astonish every reader, whose attention has not been particularly directed to this subject.

In that wonderful monument of philological research, the MITHRIDATES, begun by the illustrious Professor *Adelung*, and continued and augmented by the celebrated Professor *Vater*, by the Honourable *Frederick Adelung*, (the distinguished relative of the late professor,) and by the learned Baron *William von Humboldt*, we find "a delineation of the grammatical character of *thirty-four* American languages, and the Lord's Prayer in *fifty-nine*

* *Directions* prefixed to his *Key into the Languages of America. Williams* also, in speaking of their *numerals*, says, "'tis admirable how quick they are in casting up *great numbers* with the helpe of graines of corne," &c. *Key*, chap. iv.

different idioms or dialects of the savages of this country."* But what will be the reader's astonishment to learn, that since the publication of the *Mithridates*, the present learned *Adelung* has been enabled to make a more extensive survey of the languages of the globe than was before practicable, and has enumerated in *America twelve hundred and fourteen* different dialects!† Justly may we (to adopt the sentiment of Mr. Du Ponceau) express our astonishment at the great knowledge which the Literati of Europe appear to possess of America, and of the customs, manners and languages of its original inhabitants; and cheerfully ought we to express our "thanks to the Germans and Russians, our masters," to whom "the general science of languages is peculiarly indebted for the great progress that it has lately made."

The vast field of investigation, which is thus opening to our view, would be sufficient to dishearten the most adventurous and resolute philologist, if the *American* dialects were subject to the intricate anomalies of the European tongues,‡ and if they were, moreover, as ma-

* *Report*, in *Histor. Transact.* vol. i. p. xxxii.

† *Uebersicht aller bekannten Sprachen und ihrer Dialekte ;* or, *View of all the known Languages and their Dialects,* 8vo. St. Petersburg, 1820. A copy of this important work has been presented by the learned author to the American Academy of Arts and Sciences. The *Historical Transactions,* and particularly the labours of Mr. *Du Ponceau,* are noticed by the author in terms of just commendation. In connection with the example of the learned Adelung, I cannot forbear mentioning, as an incitement to American scholars, in these researches, that of Baron *William von Humboldt ;* who (as an obliging correspondent in Germany justly observes) "unites to his high rank as a politician and nobleman the distinctions of genius and erudition." This eminent philologist, (says Mr. Du Ponceau) "surrounded with the honours and dignities of his country, made a journey into the mountains of Biscay and resided there some months for the sole purpose of studying the Basque Language." *Report,* p. xxxi. He has also been engaged for some years in the study of the Languages of AMERICA.

‡ The almost inconceivable degree of regularity in the American languages is not the least curious of their peculiarities. *Molina* says of that of *Chili*— "What is truly surprising in this language is, that it contains *no irregular verb or noun.* Every thing in it may be said to be regulated with a geometrical precision, and displays much art with great simplicity, and a connection so well ordered and unvarying in its grammatical rules, which always make the subsequent depend upon the antecedent, that *the theory of the language is easy and may be learned in a few days.*" Vol. ii. p. 5, *Amer. edit.* Mr. Heckewelder observes of the *Delaware,* that the verbs are conjugated through all their negative, causative and various other forms, *with fewer irregularities than any other language that I know of.*" *Correspondence,* Letter x. Mr. *Du Ponceau* says too, of the same language, that "it would rather appear to have been formed by philosophers in their closets, than by savages in the wilderness." *Report,* p. xxvi.

ny have erroneously supposed, for the most part radically different languages. This last unfounded opinion, which has been too much countenanced by speculative writers, has doubtless been one reason why our scholars have not directed their attention to this part of American history; for, in the works of most writers upon this country, we meet with such numbers of Indian names, often ill-defined and as often misapplied, that we become perplexed and distracted with the multifarious group : Just as an uninstructed spectator (to adopt a remark applied on another occasion) who gazes on the endless variety of flowers that adorn the earth, or the innumerable stars that glitter in the heavens, is lost in the irregularity and disorder which seem to pervade those parts of the natural world, and despondingly imagines the knowledge of them to be placed beyond the reach of human attainment. But as we are enabled by the labours of a Newton and a Linnæus to class and systematize the innumerable subjects of those departments of knowledge, and find order and regularity amidst the apparent confusion, so, by the assistance of the Adelungs and Vaters and Humboldts of the old world, and of their zealous fellow-labourers in our own country, we can class and arrange the various languages spoken by man ; and thus dissipate the confusion and perplexity which reign through the chaos, and discover, in this, the like wonderful connexion and harmony, which are conspicuous in all other parts of the creation.

We now accordingly find, that the numerous dialects of *North* America may probably be reduced to three, or at most four classes or families :

1. The *Karalit*, or language of *Greenland and the Eskimaux :* *
2. The *Delaware ;* and

---

* Mr. Du Ponceau informs me in a late letter, that he is now able to establish the correctness of Professor Vater's important remark—that this *American* language is also spoken in *Asia*, by the tribe of Tartars called the *Sedentary Tschuktschi*, who inhabit the most eastern peninsula of the other continent. See *Mithridates*, vol. iij. part 3, p. 464,

3. The *Iroquois ;* to which should be added, as Mr
Heckewelder is inclined to think,
4. The *Floridian* class, comprehending the body of languages spoken on the whole southern frontier of
the United States.

By the study of only three or four original languages,
therefore, a scholar will be able to command a knowledge of the numerous dialects which are spread over all
that part of America in which our countrymen will feel
the greatest interest.   In the same manner as, by the
knowledge of three or four principal languages of the
old continent, we are able to master all the dialects which
are to be found from the northern to the southern ex-
tremities of Europe.
The *Massachusetts Historical Society*, with the view
of co-operating at this time with their brethren of other
states in affording such aid as may be in their power to
persons engaged in these interesting researches, will de-
vote a portion of their *Collections* to this part of American history ; in the course of which it is their intention
to communicate to the publick all rare and valuable me-
morials of the Indian languages, whether printed or in
manuscript, which may come into their possession.   It
is several years since they republished the principal part
of Roger Williams' small but valuable Vocabulary of the
Naraganset dialect.*   They now resume this depart-
ment of their work by the republication of the present
Grammar of the *Massachusetts* Language.   This Grammar had become so rare, that the Society had not one perfect *printed* copy of it in their extensive collection of early
American publications ; and they have been indebted to
their obliging and indefatigable correspondent, Mr. Du
Ponceau, for a *manuscript* copy, which he has liberally
presented to them.   The present republication, however,
is made from a *printed* copy belonging to one of their
members.   The Society is also indebted to Mr. Du Ponceau for the *Remarks* subjoined to the present edition,

* See vols. iii. and v.

which are distinguished by his name : The few other additions to it have been made by the editor ; to whose care his colleagues on the *Publishing Committee* have confided this part of the present volume.

It was thought proper to resume the *Indian* publications of the Society with a *Grammar* of some one of the dialects, in order that our scholars might at once be provided with a guide to direct them in their first inquiries ; and the Committee have been led by their respect for the memory of the author (and perhaps too by an excusable partiality for a New England production) to select that of *Eliot ;* which appears to have been the first ever published in *North America.** The work itself possesses great merit in many respects ; and, with the aid of Mr. Du Ponceau's remarks, it will afford essential aid in the prosecution of these studies.

But it is now proper to submit a few remarks more immediately relative to the particular language which is the subject of the present Grammar ; in doing which it will be necessary to take a general view of the other New England dialects.

The principal nations of Indians in *New England,* at the first settlement of the country by our ancestors, were five :

1. The *Pequots ;* who inhabited the most *southerly* part, which comprehended what is now the State of Connecticut. They were once "a very warlike and potent people."†
2. The *Naragansets ;* who possessed the country about Naraganset Bay, including Rhode Island and other islands in that bay, and also a part of the State of

* In *Spanish* America, grammars and dictionaries of the native languages had been published a century before Eliot's. Among the valuable books on this subject in the library of Baron W. von Humboldt, of which the editor has a list, there is a *Vocabulary of the Spanish and Mexican Languages,* printed at Mexico, as early as 1571.

† Gookin's Historical Collections of the Indians in New England ; written in 1674, and first published from the MS. in the Massachusetts Histor. Collect. vol. i. p. 147—8.

Connecticut.   This tribe is spoken of by our early historians as " a great people."*

3. The *Pawkunnawkuts ;* inhabiting the territory of the old Colony of Plymouth. These were also known by the name of *Wampanoags,* and were once in possession of Rhode Island.†

4. The *Massachusetts* Indians ; occupying principally the territory which was afterwards inhabited by the English, on Massachusetts Bay. They are described as " a numerous and great people."

5. The *Pawtuckets ;* who dwelt north and east of the Massachusetts Indians.‡

Besides these five general divisions, or tribes, of the New England Indians, however, our historians often speak of smaller divisions by specifick names, within the same territory ; which smaller divisions seem to have been so distinguished, sometimes in consequence of their local situation, and sometimes on account of a slight difference of dialect.

In respect to the *languages* of these Indians, there seems to have been one principal dialect, which extended through a great part of New England, and was the basis of all the others.   *Gookin* (in 1674) says—" The Indians of the parts of *New England*, especially upon the *sea-coasts* used the *same sort* of speech and language, only with some difference in the expressions, as they differ in several countries [qu. counties ?] in England, yet so as they can *well understand one another.*   Their speech is a distinct speech from any of those used in Europe, Asia or Africa, that . ever heard of.   And some of the *inland* Indians, particularly the Mawhawks or Maquas, use such a language, that our Indians *upon the coast* do not understand.   So the Indians to the southward, upon the sea coast about Vir

* *Ibid.* See also *Roger Williams' Key ;* where the author says—" In the *Narigansct* countrey (which is the *chief people* in the land) a man shall come to many townes, some bigger, some lesser, it may be a dozen in 20 miles travel." p. 3.

† *Mass. Histor. Collect.* vol. viii. p. 159, and vol. x. p. 20, note.

‡ *Gookin, ubi supra.*

ginia, use a speech much different from those in New England."* *Roger Williams* also, who is spoken of as particularly " skilful in the Indian tongue,"† agrees, substantially, with *Gookin ;* though from his remarks we should infer, that there were more differences of dialect than Gookin's account would lead us to suppose.   Williams says—" with this [the *Naraganset* language] I have entered into the secrets of those countries wherever *English* dwell, about two hundred miles, between the French and Dutch Plantations;" and he adds, that " there is a *mixture* of this language *North and South* from the place of my abode about *six hundred* miles ;   yet within the two hundred miles aforesaid their dialects doe exceedingly differ ; *yet not so, but* (within that compasse) *a man may by this helpe converse with thousands of natives* all over the countrey."   In another place Williams makes a remark which (as above observed) might lead us, at first view, to conclude, that there were many radical differences in the various dialects alluded to by him.   His words are—" The varietie of their Dialects and proper speech within thirtie or fortie miles each of other is very great."   But the example, which he subjoins in proof of this, shows that his expression is to be taken in a qualified sense, and must be considered as founded upon minute distinctions, which would not be thought to constitute " a very great varietie" of language by any person, except one whose ear had been long habituated to the niceties of some particular dialect ;   every trifling deviation from which would be as striking, as the slightest violation of the idiom of his native tongue.   He observes, that this *very great variety* of dialect will appear in this word *Anùm,* a dog, which he sets down in four of the languages, thus :

"*Anùm,* the *Cowweset*
Ayím,   the *Nariganset*   } dialect."
Arúm,   the *Qunnipiuck*
Alùm,   the *Neepmuck*

* Mass. Histor. Collect. vol. i. p. 149.
† *Gookin ;* in Mass. Histor. Collect. vol. i. p. 210.

Now, it will be at once perceived, that in three of these four examples there is no other difference of dialect, than the slight one occasioned by the very common interchange of the liquids *l, n, r ;* a difference, which, in a general view of the subject, would not be called " a very great one.''*

The observation of the old writers, that there was one principal or fundamental language throughout New England (and even beyond it) is in accordance with the remarks of later writers upon this subject ; who have taken a more extended view of these dialects than was practicable at the early period when Williams and Eliot wrote. It will suffice to refer to two writers of our own age, (one of them still living,) eminently distinguished for their skill in the Indian languages—the Rev. Dr. Edwards, whose *Observations* have been already cited, and the Rev. Mr. Heckewelder, whose *Account of the Indians and their languages* is well known to every reader. These two writers, who agree in every thing material to the present question, differ only in this circumstance, that each of them considers the particular dialect with which he happened to be most familiar, as the principal, or standard language,

---

* Williams' *Key*, chap. xvii. p. 106, London edit. of 1643 ; republished (in part) in Massa. Historical Collect. vols. iii. and v. Williams adds a remark, which is deserving of notice as a refutation of an *opinion* which at that day (as is often the case in our own) had been hastily formed upon a partial knowledge of the Indian languages : " So that (says he) although some pronounce not *L* nor *R*, yet it is the most proper dialect of other places ; *contrary to many reports.*'' *Ibid.*

This difference of dialect (which was probably the most important of any, because it is the most frequently alluded to by the old writers) is also noticed by *Eliot* in much the same manner as by Williams : " The consonants *l, n, r* (says he) have such a natural coincidence, that it is an eminent variation of their dialects. We *Massachusetts* pronounce the *n.* The *Nipmuk* Indians pronounce *l.* And the *Northern* Indians pronounce *r.* As instance :

We say   *Anúm*   (um produced) ⎫
Nipmuk,   *Alúm*   ⎬   *a dog.*''
Northern, *Arúm*   ⎭

To which he adds a remark that should not be overlooked—" So in *most words.*'' *Indian Gram.* p. 2. The *Nipmuk* Indians, (or *Neepmuck*, as Williams writes it) who are here mentioned, had their principal settlement about fifty miles south-west of Boston, on the territory now called Oxford, in the county of Worcester ; but their territory extended into the borders of Connecticut. *See Massa. Histor. Collect.* vol. ix. p. 80, *note.*

and then compares all the rest with that; just as an *Englishman* would make his own language the standard with which he would compare the *northern* dialects of Europe, or as a native of Italy would take the Italian language as the standard for those of the south of Europe. Thus Dr. *Edwards*, for example, in speaking of the *Mohegan* tongue, observes—"*This* language is spoken by *all the Indians throughout New England.* Every tribe, as that of Stockbridge, that of Farmington, that of New London, &c. has a different dialect; but the language is *radically the same.* Mr. Eliot's translation of the Bible is in a particular dialect of *this* language. *This* language appears to be much more extensive than any other language in North America. The languages of the Delawares in Pennsylvania, of the Penobscots bordering on Nova Scotia, of the Indians of St. Francis in Canada, of the Shawanese on the Ohio, and of the Chippewaus at the westward of Lake Huron, *are all radically the same* with the Mohegan . . . . That the languages of the several tribes in New England, of the Delawares, and of Mr. Eliot's Bible, are radically the same with the Mohegan, *I assert from my own knowledge.*"[*]

To the same effect are the observations of Mr. *Heckewelder* respecting the *Delaware* language, more properly called the *Lenni Lenape.* "The Lenni Lenape or Delawares (says he) are the head of a great family of Indian nations who are known among themselves by the generick name of *Wapanachki* or *Men of the East.* The *same language* is spread among them all in various dialects, of which I conceive the purest is that of the chief nation, the Lenape, at whose residence the great national councils meet, and whom the others, by way of respect, call *Grandfather.*"[†] In another place he says, that "this is the most widely extended language of any of those that are spoken on this side of the Mississippi. It prevails in the extensive regions of Canada, from the coast of Labrador to the mouth of Albany River, which falls into the

[*] Edwards' Observations, p. 5.
[†] Correspondence with Mr. Du Ponceau, *Letter* xiv. (Transactions, p. 391.)

southernmost part of Hudson's Bay, and from thence to the Lake of the Woods, which forms the north-western boundary of the United States. It appears to be the language of all the Indians of that extensive country, except those of the *Iroquois* stock, which are by far the least numerous . . . Out of the limits of Canada few Iroquois are found, except the remnants of those who were once settled in the vicinity of the great lakes in the northern parts of the now State of New York. There are yet some Wyandots in the vicinity of Detroit. All the rest of the Indians who now inhabit this country to the Mississippi, *are of the Lenape stock and speak dialects of that language.* It is certain, that at the time of the arrival of the Europeans, they were in possession of all the *coast* from the northernmost point of Nova Scotia to the Roanoke. Hence they were called *Wapanachki* or the *Abenaki, Men of the East.*" He adds—" In the *interior* of the country we find *every where* the Lenape and their kindred tribes."*

From these different accounts, then, it appears, that the Lenape may properly enough be considered as the principal, or standard language of the *New England Indians,* as well as of various tribes that inhabited the adjacent territories. It appears too, from the concurring testimony of our early historians, that among the Indians of *New England* there was "a great and numerous people," well known and commonly distinguished by the name of the *Massachusetts* Indians, who resided principally on the sea coast of the present State of Massachusetts, the extent of whose territory, however, was probably not very well defined. The editor, therefore, without regarding any of the subdivisions of this nation, (subdivisions, which have given rise to a variety of appellations both for the different portions of the people and for their slightly differing dialects,) has thought it proper to follow the example of *Eliot* in applying to the prevailing dialect of that people the general name of the *Massachusetts Language.* In the same manner, as we include under the general

* Heckewelder's Historical Account of the Indians, chap. ix. (in Transactions of the Histor. and Literar. Committee, &c. p. 106, 107.)

name of *English*, all the provincial dialects spoken in the several counties of England ; though, as far as we can judge, those *county* dialects differ much more from standard English, than the local dialects of Massachusetts did from the standard Indian of the country. This same language is often mentioned by our early writers under different names; sometimes under the very indefinite appellation of the *Indian language;* sometimes, however, it is called by its proper name, the *Massachusetts;* it has also been called the *Nonantum* language ; but more frequently the *Natick* tongue, apparently from the accidental circumstance, that Eliot established his first *Indian church* in the town called *Natick*, which was near Boston and was once the town of greatest note among the Indians in this quarter.

With these remarks the editor submits the present edition of this Grammar to the publick, as part of a series of scarce tracts respecting the *Indian Languages*, which it is the intention of the Historical Society to publish, from time to time, as circumstances shall permit. The present publication will probably be followed by a valuable *English and Indian Vocabulary* (of the *Massachusetts* language also) composed by Josiah Cotton, Esquire, who was the son of John Cotton and was once an occasional preacher among the Indians ; he died at *Plymouth*, in this State, during the year 1756. The MS. bears the date of the years 1707 and 1708. They also hope to obtain a Vocabulary of the language spoken at the present day by the small tribe of Indians called the *Penobscots*, who reside near the river of that name, in the State of Maine. A vocabulary of this dialect (the *Abnaki*) will be of use in making a comparison of the present language with the same dialect as we find it in Father *Râle's* MS. Dictionary, which was formed a century ago. This last work, of which a short bibliographical account was given, by the editor, in the fourth volume of the American Academy's Memoirs, page 358, and which is the greatest treasure of *Indian*, that is to be found in this part of our country, ought also to be published without delay, lest some accident should deprive us of it forever. But its large size

4

alone, even if the MS. were the property of the Historica
Society, would forbid its publication in these volumes
It is to be hoped, however, that measures will be taken
without loss of time, either under the direction of the Uni-
versity, (to whose library it belongs) or of the American
Academy of Arts and Sciences to effect its publication.

The editor has thought it might be acceptable to most
readers, and not without use, to add to this preface, an
account of the *Indian publications* made by *Eliot;* and
the following List, which has been collected from the
preceding volumes of the Historical Collections, is accordingly subjoined.   A valuable account of the *Life* of
the venerable author, drawn up by his much respected
descendant, the late Dr. John Eliot, Corresponding Se-
cretary of the Society, will be found in the eighth volume
of these Collections, and also in the *New England Bio-
graphical Dictionary* of the same writer.

JOHN PICKERING.

Salem, Massachusetts,
   July 31, 1821.

List of Eliot's Indian Publications.

1. The *Bible;* of which the *New Testament* was finished Sept. 5
   1661, (See Mass. Hist. Coll. vol. i. p. 176.) and the *Old Testament* in 1663.   The second edition of the *New* Test. was published in 1680, and of the *Old* Test. in 1685.   Eliot, in a letter
   of July 7, 1688, to the celebrated Sir Robert Boyle, who was
   Governour of the Corporation for propagating the gospel among
   the Indians of New England, and occasionally supplied money
   for that purpose, speaks of having paid ten pounds to Mr. *John
   Cotton,* " who (says he) helped me much in the *second* edition of
   the Bible."   See *Mass. Hist. Coll.* vol. iii. p. 187.—The translation of the New Testament was dedicated to King Charles
   the IId; a copy of the " Epistle Dedicatory" may be seen in
   the *Mass. Hist. Coll.* vol. i. p. 174.
2. Indian Catechisms ; several of them.—*See vol. i.* 172, *and viii.* 33.
3. ———— Grammar ; which is printed in some editions of the Bible.—
   See vol. viii. 12 and 33.
4. - —— Psalter.—*Ibid.*
5. Singing Psalms.—See vol. i. 172.
6. The Practice of Piety, published in 1686.—See a letter from Eliot
   to Boyle, in vol. iii. p. 187.
7. Baxter's Call to the Unconverted.—*See vol. i.* 172.

THE
INDIAN GRAMMAR BEGUN:

OR,

AN ESSAY TO BRING THE INDIAN LANGUAGE

INTO

RULES,

FOR THE HELP OF SUCH AS DESIRE TO LEARN THE SAME, FOR
THE FURTHERANCE OF THE GOSPEL AMONG THEM.

BY JOHN ELIOT.

Isa. 33. 19. *Thou shalt not see a fierce people, a people of a deeper speech than thou canst perceive, of a stammering tongue, that thou canst not understand.*

Isa. 66. 18. *It shall come that I will gather all Nations and Tongues, and they shall come and see my Glory.*

Dan. 7. 14. *And there was given him Dominion, and Glory, and a Kingdome, that all People, Nations and Languages should serve him, &c.*

Psal. 19. 3. *There is no speech nor language where their voice is not heard.*

Mal. 3. 11. *From the rising of the Sun, even to the going down of the same, my Name shall be great among the Gentiles, &c.*

CAMBRIDGE :

PRINTED BY MARMADUKE JOHNSON.

1666.

ROBERT BOYLE, ESQ;

GOVERNOUR:

WITH THE REST OF THE RIGHT HONOURABLE AND CHRISTIAN

CORPORATION

FOR THE PROPAGATION OF THE GOSPEL UNTO

THE INDIANS IN NEW-ENGLAND.

NOBLE SIR,

*Y*OU *were pleased, among other Testimonies of your Christian and prudent care for the effectual Progress of this great Work of the Lord Jesus among the Inhabitants of these Ends of the Earth, and goings down of the Sun,* to Command me (*for such an aspect have your so wise and seasonable Motions, to my heart*) *to Compile a* Grammar *of this Language, for the help of others who have an heart to study and learn the same, for the sake of Christ, and of the poor Souls of these Ruines of Mankinde, among whom the Lord is now about a Resurrection-work, to call them into his holy Kingdome. I have made an* Essay *unto this difficult Service, and laid together some* Bones *and* Ribs *preparatory at least for such a work. It is not worthy the Name of a* Grammar, *but such as it is, I humbly present it*

to your Honours, and request your Animadversions upo
the Work, and Prayers unto the Lord for blessing upon o
Essayes and Endeavours for the promoting of his Glor
and the Salvation of the Souls of these poor People.   Th
humbly commending your Honours unto the blessing o
Heaven and to the guidance of the Word of God, which
able to save your Souls, **I remain**

> **Your Honours Servant in the Service**
> **of our Lord Jesus,**
> *JOHN ELIOT.*

THE

INDIAN GRAMMAR BEGUN.

—

GRAMMAR is the *Art* or *Rule of Speaking*.

There be two parts of *Grammar :*
1. The *Art* of *making words*.
2. The *Art* of *ordering words* for speech.

The art of *making* { 1. By various *articulate sounds*.
words, is { 2. By *regular composing* of them.

Articulate sounds are composed into { *Syllables*.
{ *Words*.

The various *articulate sounds* must be distinguished
By { *Names*.
{ *Characters*.

These *Names* and *Characters* do make the *Alpha-bet*.

Because the *English Language* is the first, and most attainable Language which the *Indians* learn, he is a learned man among them, who can *Speak, Reade* and *Write* the *English Tongue*.

I therefore use the same *Characters* which are of most common use in our English Books ; *viz.* the *Roman* and *Italick* Letters.

Also our *Alpha-bet* is the same with the *English*, saving in these few things following.

1. The *difficulty of the Rule* about the Letter [*c*], by reason of the *change of its sound* in the five sounds, *cå ce ci co cu ;* being sufficiently helped by the Letters [*k* and *s*.] : We therefore lay by the Letter [*c*], [p. 2.]

saving in [ch]; of which there is frequent use in the La
guage.   Yet I do not put it out of the *Alpha-bet*, for t
use of it in other Languages, but the Character [ch] ne
to it, and call it [chee].

2. I put [i] Consonant into our *Alpha-bet*, and give
this Character [j], and call it *ji* or [gi], as this Syllal
soundeth in the English word [giant]; and I place
next after [i vocal].   And I have done thus, because
is a *regular sound* in the *third person singular* in the *Imp
ative Mode* of Verbs, which cannot well be distinguis
ed without it; though I have sometimes used [gh]
stead of it, but it is harder and more inconvenient.   T
proper sound of it is, as the English word [*age*] soun
eth.   See it used *Genes.* 1. 3, 6, 9, 11.

3. We give (v) Consonant a *distinct name*, by putti
together (*ŭ f*) or (*uph*), and we never use it, save wh
it soundeth as it doth in the word (*save, have*), and pla
it next after (*u* vocal.)   Both these Letters (*u* Voc
and *v* Consonant) are together in their proper sounds
the Latine word (*uva* a Vine.)

4. We call *w* (*wee*), because our name giveth no h
of the *power* of its sound.

These Consonants (*l. n. r.*) have such a *natural coin
dence*, that it is an eminent variation of their dialects.

We *Massachusetts* pronounce the *n*.   The *Nipm*
Indians pronounce *l*.   And the *Northern Indians* pr
nounce *r*.   As instance :

We say   *Anŭm*   (*um* produced ⎫
Nipmuk,   *Alŭm*   ⎬ A Dog.
Northern,   *Arŭm*   ⎭ So in most wor

Our *Vocals* are five : *a e i o u.*   *Dipthongs*, or d
ble sounds, are many, and of much use.

ai   au   ei   ee   eu   eau   oi   oo   ∞.

Especially we have more frequent use of [o *and*
than other Languages have : and our [∞] doth alwa
sound as it doth in these English words (*moody, book.*

We use onely *two Accents*, and but *sometime.* [p. 3.]
The *Acute* (´) to shew which Syllable is first
produced in pronouncing of the word ; which if it be not
attended, no Nation can understand their own Language :
as appeareth by the *witty Conceit* of the *Tytere tu's.*

ó produced with the accent, is a *regular distinction* betwixt the *first* and *second persons plural* of the *Suppositive
Mode ;* as

{ Naumog, *If we see :*   (as in *Log.*)
{ Naumóg, *If ye see :*   (as in *Vogue.*)

The other *Accent* is (^), which I call *Nasal ;* and it is
used onely upon (ô) when it is sounded in the Nose, as
oft it is ; or upon (ä) for the like cause.

This is a *general Rule*, When two (o o) come together, ordinarily the *first* is *produced ;* and so when two (∞)
are together.

All the *Articulate sounds* and *Syllables* that ever I heard
(with observation) in their Language, are sufficiently
comprehended and ordered by our *Alpha-bet*, and the
Rules here set down.

Character.	*Name.*	*Character.*	*Name.*
a		n	en
b	bee	o	
c	see	p	pee
ch	chee	q	keúh
d	dee	r	ar
e		ſ s	es
f	ef	t	tee
g	gee *as in* geese	u	
h		v	vf
i		w	wee
j	ji *as in* giant	x	ex
k	ka	y	wy
l	el	z	zad.
m	em		

Here be **27** *Characters :* The reason of *increasing the
number* is above.

5

And I have been thus far bold with the *Alpha-bet,*
cause it is the first time of *writing this Language ;*
it is better to settle our *Foundation* right at first, than
have it to *mend afterwards.*

[p. 4.]   *Musical sounds* they also have, and *per*
Harmony, but they differ from us in *sound.*

There be four several sorts of *Sounds* or *Tones* utt
ed by Mankinde.

1. *Articulation* in Speech.
2. *Laughter.*
3. *Lætation* and *Joy :* of which kinde of *sounds*
   Musick and *Song* is made.
4. *Ululation, Howling, Yelling,* or *Mourning :* a
   of that kinde of *sound* is their *Musick* a
   Song made.

In which kinde of *sound* they also *hallow* and c
when they are most vociferous.

And that it is thus, it may be perceived by this, th
their Language is so full of (∞) and ô *Nasal.*

They have *Harmony* and *Tunes* which they sing, b
the matter is not in *Meeter.*

They are much pleased to have their Language a
Words in *Meeter* and *Rithme,* as it now is in *The Sin*
ing Psalms in some poor measure, enough to *begin* a
break the ice withall : These they sing in our *Music*
Tone.

So much *for the* Sounds *and* Characters.

———

Now follows the Consideration of Syllables, *and*
the Art *of* Spelling.

THE *formation of Syllables* in their Language, doth
nothing differ from the *formation of Syllables* in the E
glish, and other *Languages.*

When I taught our *Indians* first to lay out a Word i
to *Syllables,* and then according to the *sound* of ever
Syllable to make it up with the *right Letters,* viz. if
were a *simple sound,* then *one Vocall* made the Syllable

if it were such a *sound* as required some of the *Consonants* to make it up, then the *adding* of the *right Consonants* either *before* the Vocall, or *after* it, or *both*. They quickly apprehended and understood this *Epitomie* of the *Art of Spelling*, and could soon learn to *Reade*.

The *Men, Women*, and *up-grown Youth* do thus [p. 5.] rationally learn to **Reade**: but the *Children* learn by *rote* and *custome*, as other Children do.

Such as desire to learn this Language, must be attentive to *pronounce right*, especially to produce *that Syllable* that is *first to be produced ;* then they must *Spell* by Art, and accustome their *tongues* to pronounce their *Syllables* and *Words ;* then learn to reade such *Books* as are Printed in their Language. *Legendo, Scribendo, Loquendo*, are the *three means* to learn a Language.

So much for the Rule *of* Making Words.

———

Now follows the Ordering *of them for* Speech.

THE several sorts of words are called *Parts of Speech*, which are in number *Seven*.

1. The *Pronoun.*
2. The *Noun.* 3. The *Adnoun*, or *Adjective.*
4. The *Verb.* 5. The *Adverb.*
6. The *Conjunction.*
7. The *Interjection.*

Touching these several kindes of Words, we are to consider,

1. The *formation* of them *asunder* by themselves.
2. The *construction* of them, or the laying them together, to make *Sense*, or *a Sentence*.

And thus far *Grammar* goeth in concatenation with *Logick :* for there is a *Reason of Grammar*. The *laying of Sentences* together to make up a *Speech*, is performed by *Logick :* The *adorning* of that Speech with *Elo-*

quence, is performed by *Rhetorick.* Such a *use* and
cord there is in these *general Arts.*

In the *formation* of words *asunder* by themselves,

Consider
{
1. The *general Qualifications,* or *Affection*
   words.
2. The *Kindes* of Words.

[p. 6.]'

The *Qualifications* are
{
1. In respect of their *A*
   whence they spring.
2. In respect of their *Conse*
   how they are yoked.

In respect of their
Rise some are
{
1. *Original words : suæ originis.*
2. *Ort words* sprung out of othe
   Chiefly {
   Nominals : or *Verbs* m
   out of *Nouns.*
   Verbals : or *Nouns* m
   out of *Verbs.*

In respect of *Consorts,*
some are
{
Simple words : one alone.
Compounded words : when
   or more are made into or

This Language doth greatly delight in *Compoun*
of words, for Abbreviation, to *speak much* in *few wo*
though they be sometimes *long ;* which is chiefly cau
by the *many Syllables* which the *Grammar Rule* requi
and *suppletive Syllables* which are of no signification,
curious care of *Euphonie.*

So much for the common Affection of words.

—

Now follow the severall Kindes *of words.*

THERE be two
kindes :
{
1. *Chief leading* { *Nouns.*
   words ;   { *Verbs.*
2. Such as *attend upon,* and belong
   unto the *chief leading words.*

	1. Such as are *proper*	*Adnouns.*
Attendants on the	to each ; as	*Adverbs.*
Chief, are	2. Such as are of *com-*	*Pronouns.*
	mon use to both ; as	*Conjunctions.*

Independent Passions or *Interjections* come under   [p. 7.]
no *Series* or *Order*, but are of use in Speech, to
express the *passionate minde* of man.

Touching the *principal parts of Speech*, this may be said
in general, That *Nouns* are the *names of Things*, and
Verbs are the *names of Actions ;* and therefore their *proper Attendants* are answerable. *Adnouns* are the *qualities of Things*, and *Adverbs* are the *qualities of Actions.*

And hence is that wise Saying, *That a Christian must
be adorned with as many Adverbs as Adjectives :* He must
as well *do good*, as *be good.* When a man's virtuous
Actions are well adorned with *Adverbs*, every one will
conclude that the man is well adorned with virtuous
Adjectives.

---

1. *Of the Pronoun.*

BECAUSE of the common and general use of the *Pronoun* to be affixed unto both *Nouns*, *Verbs* and other *parts
of Speech*, and that in the *formation* of them; therefore
that is the *first Part of Speech* to be handled.

I shall give no other description of them but this, They
are such words as do express all the *persons*, both *singular*
and *plural :* as

Sing.	Neen	*I.*	*Plu.*	Neenawun *or* kenawun,	*We.*
	Ken	*Thou*		Kenaau Ye.	
	Noh *or* nagum	*He.*		Nahoh *or* Nagoh,	*They.*

There be also other *Pronouns* of frequent use :

As the *Interrogative* of *persons :* sing. Howan. pl. Howanig, *Who.*

The *Interrogative* of *things ;*   sing. Uttiyeu, *or* tanyeu.
                              pl. Uttiyeush, *Which.*

Demonstratives {
of persons : {
sing. Ycuoh, *This or that man.* Noh
pl. Yeug, *These men.* Nag or neg, *They.*
}
of things : {
Ycu *This.* Ne *This.*
Ycush *These.* Nish *These.*
}
}

[p. 8.]

Distributives ; as { Nawhutchee, *some.* Monaog, *many.* } { Tohsuog ? Tohsunash } *How many*

But because these are not of use in *affixing* to other *Parts of Speech*, they may as well be reckoned among *Adnouns*, as some do ; though there is another *Schesis* upon them, and they attend upon *Verbs* as well as *Nouns*.

The *first* and *second persons* are of most use in affixing both of *Nouns* and *Verbs*, and other Parts of Speech.

The *third person singular* is affixed with such Syllables as these, Wut. wun. um. ∞. &c. having respect to *Euphonie :* And sometime the *third person*, especially of *Verbs* hath no *affix.*

These *Pronouns*, (Neen *and* Ken) when they are affixed, they are *contracted into* Ne *and* Ke, and varied in the *Vocal* or *Vowel* according to *Euphonie*, with the word it is affixed unto ; *as* N∞, K∞, &c.

If the word unto which it is affixed begin with a *Vocal* then a *Consonant* of a fitting sound is interposed, to couple the *word* and his *affix* with an Euphonie : *as* Nut. kut. num. kum, &c.

I give not *Examples* of these *Rules*, because they will be so obvious anon, when you see Nouns and Verbs *affixed.*

---

2. *Of a Noun.*

A NOUN is a *Part of Speech* which signifieth *a thing ;* or it is the *name of a thing.*

The *variation* of Nouns is not by *Male* and *Female*, as in other Learned Languages, and in *European Nations* they do.

Nor are they *varied* by *Cases, Cadencies,* and *Endings :* herein they are more like to the *Hebrew.*

Yet there seemeth to be one *Cadency* or *Case* of the *first Declination* of the *form Animate,* which endeth in *oh, uh,* or *ah ;* viz. when an *animate Noun* followeth a *Verb transitive* whose *object* that he acteth upon is *without himself.* For Example : *Gen.* 1. 16. the last word is *anogqsog,* stars. It is an *Erratum :* it should be *anogqsoh ;* because it followeth the Verb *agim,* He made. Though it be an *Erratum* in the Press, it is the fitter in some respects for an Example.   [p. 9.]

In *Nouns,* consider $\begin{cases} 1.\ \textit{Genera, or kindes of Nouns.} \\ 2.\ \textit{The qualities or affections thereof.} \end{cases}$

The *kindes* of Nouns are *two ;* according to which there be *two Declensions* of Nouns, for the variation of the number.

Numbers are two : *Singular* and *Plural.*

The first *kinde* of Nouns is, when the *thing signified* is *a living Creature.*

The second *kinde* is, when the *thing signified* is *not a living Creature.*

Therefore I order them thus :

There be two *forms* or *declensions* of Nouns : $\begin{cases} \textit{Animate.} \\ \textit{Inanimate.} \end{cases}$

The *Animate form* or *declension* is, when the *thing signified* is a living Creature : and such Nouns do alwayes make their Plural in (*og*) *; as,*

Wosketomp, *Man.* Wosketompaog. (*a*) is but for *Eupho-*
Mittamwossis, *A Woman.* Mittamwossissog.   [*nie.*
Nunkomp, *A young Man.* Nunkompaog.
Nunksqau, *A Girl.* Nunksqauog.
Englishman. Englishmanog.
Englishwoman. Englishwomanog.
So Manit, *God.* Manittoog.
Mattannit, *The Devil.* Mattannittoog.
So Ox, Oxesog. Horse, Horsesog.

The Stars they put in this form :

Anogqs, *A Star.*   Anogqsog.
Muhhog, *The Body.*   Muhhogkooog.
Psukses, *A little Bird.*   Psuksesog.
Ahtuk, *A Deer.*   Ahtuhquog.
Mukquoshim, *A Wolf.*   Mukquoshimwog.
Mosq, *A Bear.*   Mosquog.
Tummunk, *The Beaver.*   Tummunkquaog.
Puppinashim, *A Beast.*   Puppinashimwog.
Askook, *A Snake* or *Worm.*   Askookquog.
Namohs, *A Fish.*   Namohsog.   *&c.*

Some few Exceptions I know.

[p. 10.]   2. *The Inanimate form* or *declension* of Nouns,
is when the *thing signified* is not a living Creature : and these make the Plural in *ash ;* as

Hussun, *A Stone.*   Hussunash.
Qussuk, *A Rock.*   Qussukquanash.

Of this form are all Vegitables :

Mehtug, *A Tree.*   Mehtugquash.
Moskeht, *Grass.*   Moskehtuash.

And of this form are all the parts of the Body : as

Muskesuk, *The Eye* or *Face.*   Muskesukquash.
Mehtauog, *An Ear.*   Mehtauogwash.
Meepit, *A Tooth.*   Meepitash.
Meenan, *The Tongue.*   Meenanash.
Mussissittoon, *A Lip.*   Mussissittoonash.
Muttoon, *A Mouth.*   Muttoonash.
Menutcheg, *A Hand.*   Menutchegash.
Muhpit, *An Arm.*   Muhpittenash.
Muhkont, *A Leg.*   Muhkontash.
Musseet, *The Foot.*   Musseetash.

Of this form are all Virtues, and all Vices : as

Waantamoonk, *Wisdome.*   Waantamoongash, *or* onganash.

All *Verbals* are of this *form,* which end in *onk,* and
make their Plural in *ongash,* or in *onganash.*

All *Virtues* and *Vices* (so far as at present I discern) are *Verbals*, from their *activity* and *readiness* to turn into *Verbs.*

All *Tools* and *Instruments* of *Labour, Hunting, Fishing, Fowling,* are of this *form.* All *Apparel, Housing:* All *Fruits, Rivers, Waters,* &c.

So much for the kindes of *Nounes.*

The *common Affections* or *Qualifications* are two :

{ 1. The *affixing* of the *Noun* with the *Pronoun.*
{ 2. The *ranging* them into several *Ranks.*

1. The way of *affixing* of Nouns, is the putting [p. 11.] or using of the Noun in all the *three persons,* both Singular and Plural.

This *manner of speech* being a new thing to us that know the *European* or Western Languages, it must be demonstrated to us by *Examples.*

Metah, *the Heart.*

Sing.	{ Nuttah, *my heart.*	}	*Pl.*	{ Nuttahhun, *our heart.*
	{ Kuttah, *thy heart.*	}		{ Kuttahhou, *your heart.*
	{ Wuttah, *his heart.*	}		{ Wuttahhou, *their heart.*

Menutcheg, *A Hand.*

Sing.	{ Nunnutcheg, *my hand.*	}	*P.*	{ Nunnutcheganuṅ, *our hand.*
	{ Kenutcheg, *thy hand.*	}		{ Kenutcheganoo, *your hand.*
	{ Wunnutcheg, *his hand.*	}		{ Wunnutcheganoo, *their hand.*

Sing. { Nunnutcheganash, *my hands.*
{ Kenutchegash, *or* kenutcheganash, *thy hands.*
{ Wunnutchegash *or* wunnutcheganash, *his hands.*

Plu. { Nunnutcheganunnonut, *our hands.*
{ Kenutcheganoowout, *your hands.*
{ Wunnutcheganoowout, *their hands.*

Wétu, *A House.*

Sing.	{ Neek, *my house.*	}	*Pl.*	{ Neekun, *our house.*
	{ Keek, *thy house.*	}		{ Keekou, *your house.*
	{ Week, *his house.*	}		{ Weekou, *their house.*

6

ut, in.

Sing. { Neekit, *in my house.*
Keekit, *in thy house.*
Weekit, *in his house.*

} Pl. { Neekunonut, *in our house.*
Keekuwout, *in your house.*
Weekuwout, *or* wekuwo-
[mut, *in his house.*

Hence we corrupt this word Wigwam.

So much may at present suffice for the affixing *of Nouns.*

[p. 12.]   *Now for the ranging them into ranks.*

There be *three Ranks* of Nouns ; { The *Primitive.*
The *Diminutive.*
The *Possessive.*

The same *Noun* may be used in all these *Ranks.*

The *primitive Rank* expresses *the thing as it is : as* Nunkomp, *a Youth.* Nunksqua, *a Girl.* Ox. Sheep. Horse. Pig. *So* Hassun, *a stone.* Mehtug, *a tree.* Moskeht, *grass or herb.*

2. The *diminutive Rank* of Nouns doth *lessen the thing*, and expresses it to be *a little one ;* and it is formed by *adding*, with a due Euphonie (*es*) or (*emes*) unto the *primitive Noun.* For Example, I shall use the same Nouns named in the *first Rank*, here in the *second Rank : as* Nunkompaes *or* emes. Nunksquaes *or* emes. Oxemes. Sheepsemes. Horsemes. Pigsemes. Hassunemes. Mehtugques, *or* Mehtugquemes. Moskehtuemes.

And so far as I perceive, these two endings (*es* and *emes*) are degrees of *diminution :* (*emes*) is the least.

3. The *possessive Rank* of Nouns, is when the *person* doth challenge an interest in the *thing.* Hence, as the other *Ranks* may be *affixed*, this must be *affixed with the Pronoun.*

And it is made by *adding the Syllable* (eum *or* ɷm, *or* um) according to Euphonie, unto the affixed Noun. *For Example :* Num-Manittɷm, *my God.* Nuttineneum, *my man.* Nunnunkompɷm. Nunnunksquaeum. Nutoxineum. Nusheepseum. Nuthorsesum. Nuppigsum. Nuthassunneum. Nummehtugkꝏm. Nummoskehteum. Nummoskehteumash.

Both the *primitive Noun*, and the *diminutive Noun*, may be used in the form *possessive;* as *Nutsheepsemeseum*, and the like.

Nouns may be turned into *Verbs* two wayes :

1. By turning the Noun into the Verb-substantive form : *as* Wosketompooo, *He became a man.* Of this see more in the *Verb Substantive.*

2. All *Nouns* that end in *onk*, as they come   [p. 13.] from *Verbs* by adding (*onk*) so they will turn back again into *Verbs*, by taking away (*onk*) and forming the word according to the Rule of *Verbs;* as

Waantamoonk *is Wisdome :* take away *onk*, and then it may be *formed*   Noowaantam, *I am wise.* Koowaantam, *Thou wise,* &c. Waantam, *He wise,* &c.

---

3. *Of Adnouns.*

An *Adnoun* is *a part of Speech* that *attendeth* upon a *Noun*, and signifieth *the Qualification* thereof.

The *Adnoun* is capable of both the *Animate* and *Inanimate forms;* and it agreeth with his *leading Noun*, in *form, number,* and *person.*

For example : *Rev.* 4. 4. *there is* Neesneechagkodtash nabo yau appuongash, *Twenty four Thrones. And* Neesneechagkodtog yauog Eldersog, *Twenty four Elders.* Here be two *Nouns* of the two several forms, *Animate* and *Inanimate;* and the same *Adnoun* is made to agree with them both.

The *Inanimate form* of *Adnouns* end some in *i*, and some in *e*.

The *Animate form* in *es*, or *esu :* and those are turned into *Verbs* by taking the *affix.*   As

Wompi, *White.*   Wompiyeuash.
Mœi, *Black.*   Mœescuash.
Menuhki, *Strong.*   Menuhkiyeuash.
Nœchumwi, *Weak.*   Nœchumwiyeuash.

The same words in the Animate form :

Wompesu.   Wompesuog.
Mœesu.   Mœesuog.
Menuhkesu.   Menuhkesuog.
Nœchumwesu.   Nœchumwesuog.

Put the affix *to these, and they are Verbs.*

———

[p. 14.]   NUMERALS belong unto *Adnouns,* and in them there is something remarkable.

From the Number 5 and upward, they *adde a word suppletive,* which signifieth nothing, but receiveth the Grammatical variation of the *Declension,* according to the *things* numbered, *Animate* or *Inanimate.* The *Additional* is (*tohsú*) or (*tahshé*) which is varied (*tohsúog, tohsúash,* or *tohshinash.*)

For Example :

1	*Nequt.*		6	*Nequtta tahshe.*	
2	*Neese.*		7	*Nesausuk tahshe.*	
3	*Nish.*		8	*Shwosuk tahshe.*	
4	*Yau.*		9	*Paskoogun tahshe.*	
5	*Napanna tahshe* { *tohsuog.* / *tohsuash.*		10	*Piuk. Piukqussuog, Piukqussuash.*	

Then from 10 to 20 they *adde* afore the Numeral (*nab* or *nabo*) and then it is not needful to *adde the following additional,* though sometimes they do it.

As for Example:

11	*Nabo nequt.*		16	*Nabo nequtta.*
12	*Nabo neese.*		17	*Nabo nesausuk.*
13	*Nabo nish.*		18	*Nabo shwosuk.*
14	*Nabo yau.*		19	*Nabo paskoogun.*
15	*Nabo napanna.*		20	*Neesneechag* { *kodtog.* *kodtash.* }

Then *upwards* they *adde* to *Neesneechag*, the *single Numbers* to 30, &c.

30	*Nishwinchag kodtog, kodtash.*
40	*Yauunchag kodtog, kodtash.*
50	*Napannatahshinchag kodtog, kodtash.*
60	*Nequtta tahshinchag kodtog, kodtash.*
70	*Nesausuk tahshinchag kodtog, kodtash.*
80	*Shwosuk tahshinchag kodtog, kodtash.* [p. 15.]
90	*Paskoogun tahshinchag kodtog, kodtash.*
100	*Nequt pasuk kooog. koonash.*
1000	*Nequt muttannonganog* { *kodtog.* *kodtash.* } or { *kussuog.* *kussuash.* }

The *Adnoun* is frequently *compounded* with the *Noun*, and then usually they are *contracted : as*

Womposketomp, *A white man.*
Moooosketomp, *A black man.*
Menuhkoshketomp, *A strong man,*
Menuhkekont, *A strong leg.*   Qunuhtug, *of qunni, long.*
Mehtug, *Wood* or *Tree.* And this word is used for *a Pike.*

When the *Noun* becometh a Verb, then the *Adnoun* becometh an *Adverb.*

There is no form of *comparison* that I can yet finde, but *degrees* are expressed by a word signifying *more : as* Anue menuhkesu, *More strong : And* Nano *More and more.*   Moocheke, *Much.*   Peesik or Peasik, *Small.*

4. *Of the Verb.*

A VERB is when *the thing signified* is an *Action.*

There be two sorts of Verbs.   The *Verb* { *Substantive.*
                                           Active.

The *Verb Substantive,* is when any thing hath *the signification of the Verb Substantive added to it :* as (*am, art, is, are, was, were*) &c.   *Actuall being* is above the nature of a *Noun,* and beneath the nature of a *Verb Active.*

We have no *compleat distinct word* for the *Verb Substantive,* as other *Learned Languages,* and our *English Tongue* have, but it is under a *regular composition* whereby *many words* are made *Verb Substantive.*

[p. 16.]   All may be referred to *three sorts,* so far as yet I see.

1. The *first sort* of *Verb Substantives* is made *by adding any of these Terminations to the word.* yeuoo, aoo, ooo ; with due *Euphonie :* And this is so, be the word a *Noun ; as* Wosketompoo, *He is a man :* Or *Adnoun ;* as Wompiyeuoo, *It is white :* Or be the word an *Adverb,* or the like ; as *James* 5. 12. Mattayeuoutch, *Let it be nay :* Nuxyeuoo-utch, *Let it be yea.*   The *words in the Text* are spelled with respect to *pronunciation,* more than to *Grammaticall composition :* here I spell them with respect to *Grammaticall composition.*   See more Examples of this, *Exod.* 4. 3, 4, 6, 7.

2. The *second sort* of *Verb Substantives* is when the *animate Adnoun* is made *the third person of the Verb,* and so *formed as a Verb :* as Wompesu, *White ;* Menuhkesu, *Strong ;* may be *formed as a Verb :* Noowompes, Koowompes, Wompesu.   *And so the like words.*

And of *this sort* are all *Adnouns of Vertue or Vice : as* Waantam, *Wise :* Assootu, *Foolish,* &c.

Whatever is *affirmed to be,* or *denied to be,* or if it be *asked if it be,* or expressed to be *made to be ;* All *such words* may be *Verb Substantives.*   I say, *may be,* because there be *other wayes* in the Language to express such a sense by. But it *may be thus.*

3. The *third sort* are *Verb Substantive passive,* when the *Verb Substantive* (*am, is, was,* &c.) is so annexed to a *Verb Active,* that the *person affixed* is the *object of the act;* as Nꝏwadchanit, *I am kept.*

So much for the Verb Substantive.

___

Now followeth the Verb Active.

A *Verb Active* is when the *word* signifieth *a compleat action,* or *a causall power exerted.*

Verbs inceptives or *inchoatives,* I find not; such a *notion* is expressed by *another word added to the Verb,* which signifieth *to begin,* or *to be about to do it.*

Also when the Action is *doubled,* or *frequented,* &c. this *notion* hath not a *distinct form,* but is [p. 17.] expressed by *doubling the first Syllable* of the *word:* as Mohmoeog, *they oft met;* Sasabbath-dayeu, *every Sabbath.*

There be *two sorts* or *forms* of *Verbs Active:*
{ 1. The *Simple form*
{ 2. The *Suffix form.*

The *Simple form* of the *Verb Active,* is when the *act is conversant* about a *Noun inanimate* onely: as

Nꝏwadchanumunneek, *I keep my house.*

And this *Verb* may take the *form* of an *Adnoun:* as

Nꝏwadchanumunash nꝏwéatchimineash, *I keep my corn.*

Or every *person* of this *Verb,* at least in the *Indicative Mode,* will admit the *plural Number* of the *Noun inanimate.*

The *Suffix form* of the *Verb Active,* is when the *act is conversant* about *animate Nouns* onely; or about both *animate* and *inanimate* also: as

Kꝏwadchansh, *I keep thee.*
Kꝏwadchanumoush, *I keep it for thee.*

There be *five Concordances* of the *Suffix form Active* wherein the Verb doth receive a *various formation.* I think there be some more, but I have beat out no more

The reason why I call them *Concordances*, is, Because the *chief weight* and *strength* of the *Syntaxis* of this Language, lyeth in this eminent manner of *formation of Nouns* and *Verbs*, with the *Pronoun persons.*

1.   The *first Concordance* is, when the *object of the act* is an *animate Noun.* I call it, *The Suffix animate object : as*
Koowadchansh, *I keep thee.*

2.   The *Suffix animate mutual :* when *animates* are each others *object : as*
Noowadchanittimun, *We keep each other.*
This *form* ever wanteth the *singular Number.*

3.   The *Suffix animate end,* and *inanimate object : as*
Koowadchanumoush, *I keep it for thee ; or, for thy use.*

[p. 18.]   4.   The *Suffix animate form social : as*
Kooweechewadchanumwomsh, *I keep it with thee.*

5.   The *Suffix form advocate* or *in stead form,* when one acteth in the *room* or *stead* of another : as
Koowadchanumwanshun, *I keep it for thee ;   I act in thy stead.*

This *form* is of great use in *Theologie,* to express what Christ *hath done for us : as*

Nunnuppoowonuk, *He died for me.*
Kenuppoowonuk, *He died for thee.*
Kenuppoowonukqun, *He died for us.*
Kenuppoowonukoo, *He died for you.*   &c.

All these forenamed *forms of Verbs,* both *Verb Substantives* and *Verbs Active,* both *Simple* and *Suffix,* may be varied under three *distinct forms of variation ;* viz.

{ *Affirmative :* when the *act* is *affirmed.*
{ *Negative :* when the *act* is *denied.*
{ *Interrogative :* when the *act* is *question'd.*

Again, many of these *forms* may also be varied in a *form causative*, in all cases where the *efficient* is capable to be *compelled*, or *caused to act*.

All these will be more conspicuous in the *Paradigms*, or *Examples*.

To make *compleat work*, I should set down many examples.

But I shall (at present) set down onely two examples: One of the *Simple form Active*, which may generally serve for all the *Verb Substantives*.

The *second Example* of the *Suffix animate form*, which may generally serve for all the *Concordances of Verbs suffixed.* Even as the *Meridian* of *Boston* may generally serve for all *New-England* : And the *Meridian* of *London* may generally serve for all *England*.

And these will be enough to busy the heads of *Learners* for a while.

Note this, That *all Verbs* cannot be formed [P. 19.] through *all these forms*, but such Verbs as in reason of Speech are *useable all these wayes*, which sundry Verbs are not ; as, *I sleep, eat, piss,* &c.

Before I come to the *Paradigms*, there be other general considerations about *Verbs*.

In *Verbs* consider $\begin{cases} \text{1. Divers } Modes \text{ of the } action. \\ \text{2. Divers } Times \text{ of the } action. \end{cases}$

First, The *Modes of actions* in this Language are *five*.
1. The *Indicative, Demonstrative,* or *Interrogative Mode*, which doth fully *assert the action* or *deny it*, or *enquire* if it be asserted :

As $\begin{cases} \text{N}\infty\text{wadchanumun, } I \text{ } do \text{ } keep \text{ } it. \\ \text{N}\infty\text{wadchanum}\infty\text{un, } I \text{ } do \text{ } not \text{ } keep \text{ } it. \\ \text{N}\infty\text{wadchanumunas, } Do \text{ } I \text{ } keep \text{ } it? \end{cases}$

2. The *Imperative*, or *Hortative*, or *Praying* and *Blessing Mode*, is when the *action* is *Commanded*, or *Exhorted*

7

to be done, or *Prayed* for.   When a Superiour speaks i
this *Mode*, he *commands*.   When an Inferiour speaks i
this *Mode*, he *prayes* and *intreats*.   When a Ministe
speaks in this *Mode*, he *exhorts*, and *blesseth*.

> Wadchansh, *Keep thou.*
> Wadchanch, *Keep me.*

3. The *Optative*, *Wishing*, or *Desiring Mode*, whe
one desireth the *action to be done :* as

> Nœwaadchanumun toh, *I wish or desire to keep it.*

4. The *Subjunctive*, or rather *the Supposing*, or *Sup*
positive Mode, when the *action* is onely *supposed to be ;* a
in these three expressions :

> { *If it be.*
> { *When it is.*
> { *It being.*

And this third *sense* and *meaning* of this *Mode* of th
Verb, doth turn this *Mode* into a *Participle*, like an *Ad*
noun, very frequently.

[p. 20.]   5. The *Indefinite Mode*, which doth onely as
       sert the action without *limitation* of *person* o
time ; and it is made of the *Indicative Mode* by adding
the termination (*ât*) and taking away the *suffix :* as

> Wadchanumunat, *To keep.*

There is another *Mode of the Verb* in reason of speech
and in some other Languages, *viz.* The *Potential*, which
doth render the action in *a possibility to be.*   But thi
Language hath not such a *Mode*, but that *notion* is ex
pressed by a word signifying (*may*) to the *Indicativ*
Mode.   The usual word with us is (*woh*) *may* or *can.*

All these *Modes of the Verb* are *timed* by *Tenses*, sav
ing the *Indefinite Mode*, and that is *unlimited.*

The *times* are two ; *Present*, and *Past.*   The *time t*
come is expressed by a word signifying *futurity*, added to
the *Indicative Mode, as* (mos, pish, *shall*, or *will.*)

In the *Roman Language* there do belong unto this *Indefinite Mode, gerundive, lofty,* and *vapouring* Expressions; also *supine, sluggish, dull,* and *sunk-hearted* Expressions. And though the spirit of this People, *viz.* the *vapouring pride* of some, and the *dull-hearted supinity* of others, might dispose them to such words and expressions, yet I cannot find them out.

As *Nouns* are often turned into *Verbs,* so *Verbs* are often turned into *Nouns ;* and a frequent way of it is, by adding (*onk*) to the *Verb :* as

> Nꝏwompes, *I am white.*
> Kꝏwompes, *Thou art white.*
> Nꝏwompesuonk, *My whiteness.*
> Kꝏwompesuonk, *Thy whiteness.*

Every *person of the Verb* that is capable of such a *change* in the reason of Speech, may so be turned into a *Noun* singular or plural.

Before I set down the Examples of *Formation of Verbs,* I will finish *a few Observations* about the remaining Parts of Speech.

[p. 21.]

5. *Of Adverbs.*

An *Adverb* is a word that *attendeth* upon the Verb, and signifieth *the quality of the action,* by *Extension, Diminution, Rectitude, Curvation, Duration, Cessation,* &c. according to the various qualities of all sorts of actions.

Adverbs do usually end in (*e* or *u*), as *wame* or *wamu,* All : *Menuhke* or *Menuhku,* Strongly.

The several sorts of *Adverbs* (according as Learned Grammarians have gathered them together) are

1. *Of Time.* Yeuyeu, *Now.* Wunnonkou, *Yesterday.* Saup, *To morrow.* Ahquompak, *When.* Paswu, *Lately.*

Nôadtuk, *A long time.*   Teanuk, *Presently.*   Kuttumma, *Very lately.*

2. *Of Place.* Uttiyeu, *Where.* Naut, *There.* Anomut, *Within.* Woskeche, *Without.* Onkoue, *Beyond.* Negonnu, *First.* Wuttát, *Behinde.*

3. *Of Order.* Negonnu, *First.* Nahohtôeu, *Second.* Nishwu, *Third,* &c.

4. *Of Asking.* Sun, Sunnummatta; *Is it?* or *Is it not?* Tohwutch, *Why.*

5. *Of Calling.* Hoh. Chuh.

6. *Affirming.* Nux, *Yea.* Wunnamuhkut, *Truely.*

7. *Denying.* Matta, Matchaog, *No. Also* Mo *sometimes signifieth* No. They have no *Adverbs* of *Swearing,* nor any *Oath,* that I can yet finde : onely we teach them to Swear before a Magistrate *By the great and dreadful name of the Lord.* The word we make for *swearing,* signifieth *to speak vehemently.*

8. *Of Exhorting* or *Encouraging.* Ehhoh, Hah.

9. *Of Forbidding.* Ahque, *Beware, Do not.*

10. *Of Wishing.* Woi, Napehnont, *Oh that it were.* Toh.

11. *Of Gathering together.* Moeu, *Together.* Yeu nogque, *This way-ward.* Ne nogque, *That way-ward.* Kesukquieu, *Heaven-ward.* Ohkeiyeu, *Earth-ward.*

12. *Of Choosing.* Anue, *More rather.* Teaogku, *Rather, unfinished.* Nahen, *Almost.* Asquam, *Not yet.*

[p. 22.]   13. *Of Continuation.* Ash, *Still.*

14. *Of Shewing.* Kusseh, *Behold.*

15. *Of Doubting.* Pagwodche, *It may be.* Toh, *It may be.*

16. *Of Likeness.* Netatup, *Like so.* Nemehkuh, *So.* Neane, *As.*

17. *Of unexpected Hap.* Tiadche, *Unexpectedly.*

18. *Of Quality.* Wunnegen. Matchet. Waantamwe, *&c.* *Of this kinde are all* Virtues *and* Vices, *&c.*

Adverbs are oft turned into *Adnouns,* especially when his *Verb* is turned into a *Noun.*

6. *Of the Conjunction.*

A *Conjunction* is a Part of Speech to joyn *Words* and *Sentences :* As

Causatives. Wutch, wutche, newutche. *For, from, because.* Yeu waj, *For this cause.*

Disjunctives. Asuh, *Or.*

Discretives. Qut, *But.*

Suppositives. Tohneit, *If.*

Exceptives. Ishkont, *Least.* Chaubohkish, *Except,* or *besides.* Kuttumma, *Unless.*

Diversatives. Tohkônogque, *Although.*

Of Possibility. Woh, *May* or *Can.*

Of Place. In, en, ut, át. *In, At* or *To.*

---

7. *Of Interjections.*

An *Interjection* is a *word* or *sound* that uttereth the *passion of the minde*, without dependance on other words.

Of Sorrow. Woi, oowee.

Of Marvelling. Hó, hoo.

Of Disdaining. Quah.

Of Encouraging. Hah, Ehoh.

There be also *suppletive Syllables* of no signi- [p. 23.] fication, but for *ornament* of the word : as *tit, tin, tinne ;* and these in way of an *Elegancy,* receive the *affix* which belongeth to the *Noun* or *Verb* following ; as *nuttit, kuttit, wuttit, nuttin, kuttin, wuttin, nuttinne, kuttinne, wuttinne.*

Other Languages have their *significant suppletives* for Elegancy : and some of our English Writers begin so to use [*Why*], but I conceive it to be a *mistake.* Our *suppletive* is rather [*Weh*], and [*Why*] is a *significant word.* It oft puts the Reader to this inconvenience, to stay and look whether it be significant or not ; and some are *stum-*

bled at it.   It is seldome *an Elegancy,* to make a significant word a meer suppletive.

   So much for the formation of words asunder.

For the Construction of words together, *I will give three short Rules.*

   1. WHEN *two Nouns come together,* one of them is turned into a kinde of an Adverb, or Adnoun, and that is an *Elegancy* in the Language : of which see frequent Examples.   See 1 *Pet.* 2. 2.   Pahke sogkodtungane wuttinnowaonk, *The pure milkie word,* for *milk of the word.*   The like may be observed a thousand times.

   2. When *two Verbs come together,* the latter is the *Infinitive Mode :* as in the same 1 *Pet.* 2. 5. Kooweekikonitteamwoo sephausinat. *Ye are built,* &c. *to sacrifice,* &c. And a thousand times more this Rule occurs.

   3. When a *Noun* or a *Verb* is attended upon with an *Adnoun,* or *Adverb,* the *affix* which belongeth to the Noun or Verb is *prefixed* to the Adnoun or Adverb : as in the same Chapter, 1 *Pet.* 2. 9. Ummonchanatamwe wequaiyeumut, *His marvellous light :* The affix of *Light* is prefixed to *marvellous.*   Koowaantamwe ketoohkam, *Thou speakest wisely :* The affix of *speaking* is prefixed to *wisely.*   This is a frequent Elegancy in the Language.

   But the manner of the *formation* of the *Nouns* and *Verbs* have such a *latitude of use,* that there needeth little other *Syntaxis* in the Language.

[p. 24.]   I shall now set down *Examples of Verbs :* and first of the *Simple form.*   And here
   First, I shall set down a *Verb Active,* whose object is *Inanimate :*
      as Noowadchanumun, *I keep it.*   (*Be it tool or garment.*)
And secondly, I shall set down a *Verb Substantive :*
      as Noowaantam, *I am wise.*
Both these I shall set down *Parallel* in two Columes.

The form Affirmative.

Indicative Mode.

Present tense.		Present tense.	
I keep it.		*I am wise.*	
Sing.	Noowadchanumun / Koowadchanumun / oowadchanumun.	Sing.	Noowaantam / Koowaantam / Waantam noh.
Plur.	Noowadchanumumun / Koowadchanumumwoo / Wadchanumwog.	Plur.	Noowaantamumun / Koowaantamumwoo / Waantamwog.

Præter tense.		Præter tense.	
Sing.	Noowadchanumunap / Koowadchanumunap / oowadchanumunap.	Sing.	Noowaantamup / Koowaantamup / Waantamup.
Pl.	Noowadchanumumunnônup / Koowadchanumumwop / Wadchanumuppanneg: *or* / oowadchanummuáop.	pl.	Noowaantamumunnônup / Koowaantamúmwop / Waantamuppanneg.

The *Imperative Mode,* when it *Commands* or *Exhorts* it wanteth the *first person singular:* but when we *Pray* in this *Mode,* as always we do, then it hath the *first person;* as, *Let me be wise:* but there is no formation of the word to express it; yet it may be expressed by adding this word unto the *Indicative Mode* [pâ], *as,* [p. 25. Pânoowaantam, *Let me be wise.* Our usual formation of the *Imperative Mode* is without the *first person singular,* casting away the *affix.*

Imperative Mode.

Present tense.		Present tense.	
Sing.	Wadchanish / Wadchanitch.	Sing.	Waantash / Waantaj.
plur.	Wadchanumuttuh / Wadchanumook / Wadchanumahettich.	plur.	Waantamuttuh / Waantamook / Waantamohettich.

The *Imperative Mode* cannot admit of any other *time* than the *Present.*

The *Optative Mode.*

Present tense.

Sing. { Nœwáadchánumun-toh
Kœwáadchanumun-toh
œwaadchanumun-toh.

plur. { Nœwaadchanumunnan-toh
Kœwaadchanumunnan-toh *pl.*
œwaadchanumuncau-toh.

Present tense.

Sing. { Nœwáaantamun-toh
Kœwáaantamun-toh
œwáaantamun-toh.

pl. { Nœwáaantamunan-toh
Kœwáaantamuncau-toh
œwáaantamuncau-toh

Præter tense.

Sing. { Nœwaadchanumunaz-toh
Kœwaadchanumunaz-toh
œwaadchanumunaz-toh.

Plu.

{ Nœwaadchanumunannonuz-toh
Kœwaadchanumunaóuz toh.
œwaadchanumunaóuz-toh.

Præter tense.

S. { Nœwáaantamunaz-toh
Kœwáaantamunaz-toh
œwáaantamunaz-toh.

Plu.

{ Nœwáaantamúnanôiz-toh
Kœwáaantamunaôiz-toh
œwáaantamunaôiz-toh.

It seems their desires are slow, *but* strong ;
Because they be utter'd double-breath't, *and* long.

[p. 26.]

The *Suppositive Mode :* which usually *flats* the *first Vocal* and layes by the *affix.*

Present tense.

Sing. { Wadchanumon
Wadchanuman
Wadchanuk.

plur. { Wadchanumog
Wadchanumóg
Wadchanumahettit.

Present tense.

Sing. { Waantamon
Waantaman
Waantog.

plur. { Waantamog
Waantamóg
Waantamohettit.

Præter tense.

Sing. { Wadchanumos
Wadchanumôsa
Wadchanukis.

plur. { Wadchanumogkus
Wadchanumógkus
Wadchanumahettis.

Præter tense.

Sing. { Waantamos
Waantamas
Waantogkis.

plur. { Waantamogkis
Waantamógkis
Waantamohettis.

THE INDIAN GRAMMAR BEGUN. **27**

The *Indefinite Mode.*

Wadchanumunát   Waantamunát.

Indicative Mode. The *form Negative*, which is varied from the *Affirmative* by interposing [ꝏ].

Present tense.

Sing. {
Nꝏwadchanumꝏun
Kꝏwadchanumꝏun
ꝏwadchanumꝏun.
}

plur. {
Nꝏwadchanumꝏunnonup
Kꝏwadchanumꝏwop
Wadchanumꝏog.
}

Præter tense.

Sing. {
Nꝏwadchanumꝏunap
Kꝏwadchanumꝏunap
ꝏwadchanumꝏunap.
}

Plu.

{
Nꝏwadchanumꝏunnanónup
Kꝏwadchanumꝏwop
Wadchanumꝏpanneg.
}

Present tense.

Sing. {
Nꝏwaantamꝏh
Kꝏwaantamꝏh
Waantamꝏh.
}

plur. {
Nꝏwaantamꝏmun
Kꝏwaantamꝏmwꝏ
Waantamꝏog.
}

Præter tense.

Sing. {
Nꝏwaantamꝏp
Kꝏwaantamꝏp
ꝏwaantamop.
}

Plu.

{
Nꝏwaantamꝏmunnonup
Kꝏwaantamꝏmwop
Waantamꝏpanneg.
}

[p. 27.]

The *Imperative Mode* of the *Negative simple form.*

Present tense.

Sing. {
Wadchanuhkon
Wadchanuhkitch.
}

plur. {
Wadchanumꝏuttuh
wadchanumꝏhteók
wadchanumohettekitch.
}

Present tense.

Sing. {
Waantukon
Waantukitch.
}

plur. {
Waantamꝏuttuh
waantamꝏhteók
waantamóhettekitch.
}

The *Optative Mode* is of seldome use, and very difficult, therefore I pass it by.

8

The *Suppositive Mode* of the *Simple form.*

Present tense.

Sing. { Wadchanumꝏun
Wadchanumꝏan
Wadchanꝏg.

Plur. { Wadchanumꝏog
Wadchanumꝏóg
Wadchanumꝏahettit, *or*
ꝏhetteg.]

Præter tense.

Sing. { Wadchanumꝏos
Wadchanumꝏosa
Wadchanumꝏgkis.

Plur. { Wadchanumꝏogkus
Wadchanumꝏógkus
Wadchanumꝏahettis.

Present tense.

Sing. { Waantamꝏon
Waantamꝏan
Waantamꝏg.

Plur. { Waantamꝏog
Waantamꝏóg
Waantamꝏohettit *or*
[ꝏhetteg.

Præter tense.

Sing. { Waantamꝏos
Waantamꝏas
Waantamꝏgkis.

Plur. { Waantamꝏogkus
Waantamꝏógkus
Waantamꝏohettis.

The *Indefinite Mode* of the *Simple form Negative.*

Wadchanumꝏunát   Waantamꝏunát.

The *Simple form Interrogative*, is formed onely in the *Indicative Mode:* All *Questions* are alwayes asked in this *Mode of the Verb,* and in no other; and it is *formed* by adding [*ás*] to the *Affirmative.*

Indicative Mode.

Present tense.

Sing. { Nꝏwadchanumunás
Kꝏwadchanumunás
ꝏwadchanumunáous.

Present tense.

Plur. { Nꝏwadchanumunnanonus
Kꝏwadchanumunnaóus
ꝏwadchanumunnaóus Nag.

The *Suffix form animate Affirmative.*

Here I carry in a Parallel our English Verb (Pay) that so any may distinguish betwixt what is Grammar, and what belongs to the word. And remember ever to pronounce (pay), because else you will be ready to reade it (pau). Also remember, that (Paum) is the radicall word, and all the rest is Grammar. In this remarkable way of speech, the Efficient of the Act, and the Object, and sometimes the End also, are in a regular composition comprehended in the Verb: and there is no more difficulty in it, when use hath brought our Notion to it, than there is in other Languages, if so much.

Indicative Mode. Present tense.

1 sing.
I keep thee,
Koowadchansh.
I keep him,
Noowadchan.
I keep you,
Koowadchanunumwoo.
I keep them,
Noowadchanôog.

1 plur.
I pay thee,
Kuppaumush.
I pay him,
Nuppayum.
I pay you,
Kuppaumunumwoo.
I pay them,
Nuppaumôog.

2 sing.
Thou keepest me,
Koowadchaneh.
Thou keepest him,
Koowadchan.
Thou keepest us,
Koowadchanimun.
Thou keepest them,
Koowadchanoog.

2 plur.
Thou payest me,
Kuppaumeh.
Thou payest him,
Kuppaum.
Thou payest us,
Kuppaumimun.
Thou payest them,
Kuppaumoog.

3 sing.
He keepeth me,
Noowadchanuk.
He keepeth thee,
Koowadchanuk.
He keepeth him,
oowadchanuh.
He keepeth us,
Koowadchanukqun.
He keepeth you,
Koowadchanukoo.
He keepeth them,
oowadchanuh.

3 plur.
He payeth me,
Nuppaumuk.
He payeth thee,
Kuppaumuk.
He payeth him,
Uppaumuh.
He payeth us,
Kuppaumukqun.
He payeth you,
Kuppaumukou.
He payeth them,
Uppaumuh nah.

Indicative Mode.

Present tense.   *Present tense.*

1 plur.

We keep thee,
Kœwadchanunumun.
We keep him,
nœwadchanoun.
We keep you,
kœwadchanunumun(wame)
We keep them,
nœwadchanóunonog.

We pay thee,
Kuppaumunumun.
We pay him,
nuppaumoun.
We pay you,
kuppaumunumun.
We pay them,
nuppaumounónog.

2 plur.

Ye keep me,
Kœwadchanimwœ.
Ye keep him,
kœwadchanau.
Ye keep us,
kœwadchanimun.
Ye keep them,
kœwadchanoog.

Ye pay me,
Kuppaumimwœ.
Ye pay him,
kuppaumau.
Ye pay us,
kuppaumimun.
Ye pay them,
kuppaumoog.

3 plur.

They keep me,
Nœwadchanukquog.
They keep thee,
kœwadchanukquog.
They keep him,
œwadchanouh.
They keep us,
nœwadchanukqunnonog.
They keep you,
kœwadchanukœoog.
They keep them,
œwadchanouh nah.

They pay me,
Nuppaumukquog.
They pay thee,
kuppaumukquog.
They pay him,
uppaumouh.
They pay us,
nuppaumukqunnonog.
They pay you,
kuppaumukœoog.
They pay them,
uppaumouh nah.

Indicative Mode.

Præter tense.   *Præter tense.*

1 sing.
I did keep thee,
Kꝏwadchanunup.
I did keep him,
nꝏwadchanóp.
I did keep you,
kꝏwadchanunnumwop.
I did keep them,
nꝏwadchanópanneg.

1 sing.
I did pay thee,
Kuppaumunup.
I did pay him,
nuppaumóp.
I did pay you,
kuppaumunumwop.
I did pay them,
nuppaumópanneg.

2 sing.
Thou didst keep me,
Kꝏwadchanip.
Thou didst keep him,
kꝏwadchanóp.
Thou didst keep us,
kꝏwadchanimunonup.
Thou didst keep them,
kꝏwadchanopanneg.

2 sing.
Thou didst pay me,
Kuppaumip.
Thou didst pay him,
kuppaumóp.
Thou didst pay us,
kuppaumimunonup.
Thou didst pay them,
kuppaumopanneg.

3 sing.
He did keep me,
Nꝏwadchanukup.
He did keep thee,
kꝏwadchanukup.
He did keep him,
ꝏwadchanópoh.
He did keep us,
nꝏwadchanukqunnonup.
He did keep you,
kꝏwadchanukꝏop.
He did keep them,
ꝏwadchanꝏópoh.

3 sing.
He did pay me,
Nuppaumukup.
He did pay thee,
kuppaumukup.
He did pay him,
uppaumopoh.
He did pay us,
nuppaumukqunnonup.
He did pay you,
kuppaumukꝏwop.
He did pay them,
uppaumopoh nah.

Indicative Mode.

Præter tense.

1 plur.

We did keep thee,
Koowadchaninumunonup.
We did keep him,
noowadchanóunonup.
We did keep you,
koowadchaninumunonup.
We did keep them, [neg.
noowadchanounonuppan-

2 plur.

Ye did keep me,
Koowadchanimwop.
Ye did keep him,
koowadchanuop.
Ye did keep us,
koowadchanimunonup.
Ye did keep them,
koowadchanoopanneg.

3 plur.

They did keep me,
Noowadchanukuppanneg.
They did keep thee,
koowadchanukuppanneg.
They did keep him,
oowadchananopoh.
They did keep us, [neg.
koowadchanukqunonuppan-
They did keep you,
koowadchanukoopanneg.
They did keep them,
oowadchanoopoh nah.

Præter tense.

1 plur.

We did pay thee,
kuppaumunumunonup.
We did pay him,
nuppaumounonup.
We did pay you,
kuppaumunumunonup.
We did pay them,
nuppaumounonuppanneg.

2 plur.

Ye did pay me,
Kuppaumimwop.
Ye did pay him,
kuppaumauop.
Ye did pay us,
kuppaumimunonup.
Ye did pay them,
kuppaumauopanneg.

3 plur.

They did pay me,
Nuppaumukuppaneg.
They did pay thee,
kuppaumukuppanneg.
They did pay him,
uppaumauopoh.
They did pay us, [neg
nuppaumukqunnouppan-
They did pay you,
kuppaumukoopanneg.
They did pay them,
uppaumoopoh nah.

The *Imperative Mode* of the *Suffix form animate Affirmative.*

Note, That this Mode of the Verb doth cast off the *Affix,* or *prefixed Pronoun,* using onely the *suffixed Grammaticall variations.*

Present tense.   *Present tense.*

1 sing.
- *Let me keep thee,* Wanchanunutti.
- *Let me keep him,* wadchanonti.
- *Let me keep you,* wadchanunonkqutch.
- *Let me keep them,* wadchanonti nagoh.

1 sing.
- *Let me pay thee,* Paumunutti.
- *Let me pay him,* paumonti.
- *Let me pay you,* paumunonkqutch.
- *Let me pay them,* paumonti.

2 sing.
- *Do thou keep me,* Wadchaneh.
- *Do thou keep him,* wadchan.
- *Do thou keep us,* wadchaninnean.
- *Do thou keep them,* wadchan nag.

2 sing.
- *Do thou pay me,* Paumeh.
- *Do thou pay him,* paum.
- *Do thou pay us,* pauminnean.
- *Do thou pay them,* paum.

3 sing.
- *Let him keep me,* Wadchanitch.
- *Let him keep thee,* wadchanukqush.
- *Let him keep him,* wadchanonch.
- *Let him keep us,* wadchanukqutteuh.
- *Let him keep you,* wadchanukook.
- *Let him keep them,* wanchanonch.

3 sing.
- *Let him pay me,* Paumitch.
- *Let him pay thee,* paumukqush.
- *Let him pay him,* paumonch.
- *Let him pay us,* paumukqutteuh.
- *Let him pay you,* paumukook.
- *Let him pay them,* paumonch.

Imperative Mode.

Present tense.   *Present tense.*

1 plur.
- *Let us keep thee,* Wadchanunuttuh.
- *Let us keep him,* wadchanontuh.
- *Let us keep you,* wadchanunuttuh.
- *Let us keep them,* wadchanontuh.

1 plur.
- *Let us pay thee,* Paumunuttuh.
- *Let us pay him,* paumontuh.
- *Let us pay you,* paumunuttuh.
- *Let us pay them,* paumontuh.

2 plur.
- *Do ye keep me,* Wadchanegk.
- *Do ye keep him,* Wadchanók.
- *Do ye keep us,* wadchaninnean.
- *Let us keep them,* wadchanók.

2 plur.
- *Do ye pay me,* Paumegk.
- *Do ye pay him,* paumók.
- *Do ye pay us,* pauminnean.
- *Do ye pay them,* paumók.

3 plur.
- *Let them keep me,* Wadchanukquttei *or* wadchanhettich.
- *Let them keep thee,* wadchanukqush.
- *Let them keep him,* wadchanáhettich.
- *Let them keep us,* wadchanukqutteuh.
- *Let them keep you,* wadchanukœok.
- *Let them keep them,* wadchanáhettich.

3 plur.
- *Let them pay me,* Paumukquttei, *or* Paumé hettich.
- *Let them pay thee,* paumukqush.
- *Let them pay him,* paumáhettich.
- *Let them pay us,* paumukqutteuh.
- *Let them pay you,* paumukœok.
- *Let them pay them,* paumáhettich.

The *Optative Mode* of the *Suffix form animate Affirmative.*

This Adverb (toh) *or* (napehnont) *properly signifieth* (utinam) *I wish it were. And see how naturally they annex it unto every variation of this Mode of the Verb. Note also,* That this Mode keepeth the Affix, or prefixed Pronoun.

Present tense.	*Present tense.*

1 sing.
I wish I keep thee,
Kœwaadchanunan-toh, *or* napehnont.
I wish I keep him,
Nœwaadchanun-toh.
I wish I keep you,
Kœwaadchanununeau-toh.
I wish I keep them,
Nœwaadchanôneau-toh.

1 sing.
I wish I pay thee,
Kuppapaumunun-toh.
I wish I pay him,
nuppapaumun-toh.
I wish I pay you,
kuppapaumuneau-toh.
I wish I pay them,
nuppapaumôneau-toh.

2 sing.
I wish thou keep me,
Kœwaadchanin-toh.
I wish thou keep him,
kœwaadchanon-toh.
I wish thou keep us,
kœwaadchaninneau-toh.
I wish thou keep them,
kœwaadchanonneauh-toh.

2 sing.
I wish thou pay me,
kuppapaumin-toh.
I wish thou pay him,
kuppapaumon-toh.
I wish thou pay us,
kuppapaumuneau-toh.
I wish thou pay them,
kuppapaumôneau-toh.

3 sing.
I wish he keep me,
Nœwaadchanukqun-toh.
I wish he keep thee,
kœwaadchanukqun-toh.
I wish he keep him,
œwaadchanon-toh.
I wish he keep us,
kœwaadchanukqunan-toh.
I wish he keep you,
kœwaadchanukquneau-toh.
I wish he keep them,
œwaadchanon-toh.

3 sing.
I wish he pay me,
Nuppapaumukqun-toh.
I wish he pay thee,
kuppapaumukqun-toh.
I wish he pay him,
uppapaumon-toh.
I wish he pay us,
kuppapaumukqunan-toh.
I wish he pay you,
kuppapaumukquneau-toh.
I wish he pay them,
uppapaumon-toh.

9

Optative Mode.

Present tense.   *Present tense.*

1 plur.
I wish we keep thee,
Kꝏwaadchanunan-toh.
I wish we keep him,
nꝏwaadchanonan-toh.
I wish we keep you,
kꝏwaadchanunnan-toh.
I wish we keep them,
nꝏwaadchanonan-toh.

1 plur.
I wish we pay thee,
Kuppapaumunan-toh.
I wish we pay him,
nuppapaumónan-toh.
I wish we pay you,
kuppapaumunan-toh.
I wish we pay them,
nuppapaumonan-toh.

2 plur.
I wish ye keep me,
Kꝏwaadchanuncau-toh.
I wish ye keep him,
kꝏwaadchanóncau-toh.
I wish ye keep us,
kꝏwaadchanunean-toh.
I wish ye keep them,
kꝏwaadchanóneau-toh.

2 plur.
I wish ye pay me,
Kuppapaumuneau-toh.
I wish ye pay him,
kuppapaumóneau-toh.
I wish ye pay us,
kuppapaumunean-toh.
I wish ye pay them,
kuppapaumóneau-toh.

3 plur.
I wish they keep me,
Nꝏwaadchanukquncau-toh
I wish they keep thee,
kꝏwaadchanukquncau-toh.
I wish they keep him,
ꝏwaadchanóneau-toh.
I wish they keep us,
nꝏwaadchanukqunan-toh.
I wish they keep you,
kꝏwaadchanukquncau-toh.
I wish they keep them,
ꝏwaadchanóneau-toh.

3 plur.
I wish they pay me,
Nuppapaumukquncau-t
I wish they pay thee,
kuppapaumukquncau-tc
I wish they pay him,
uppapaumóneau-toh.
I wish they pay us,
nuppapaumukqunan-tol
I wish they pay you,
kuppapaumukquncau-tc
I wish they pay them,
uppapaumóneau-toh.

Optative Mode.

Præter tense.

1 sing.

I wish I did keep thee,
Kœwaadchanununaz-toh.
I wish I did keep him,
nœwaadchanónaz-toh.
I wish I did keep you,
kœwaadchanununnaouz-
toh.
I wish I did keep them,
nœwaadchanónaóoz-toh.

2 sing.

I wish thou didst keep me,
Kœwaadchaninncaz-toh.
I wish thou didst keep him,
kœwaadchanónaz-toh.
I wish thou didst keep us,
kœwaadchanuncanonuz-
oh.
I wish thou didst keep them
kœwaadchanónaouz-toh.

3 sing.

I wish he did keep me,
Nœwaadchanukqunaz-toh.
I wish he did keep thee,
kœwaadchanukqunaz-toh.
I wish he did keep him,
œwaadchanónaz-toh.
I wish he did keep us,
nœwaadchanukqunanonuz-
toh.
I wish he did keep you,
kœwaadchanukqunnaouz-
toh.
I wish he did keep them,
œwaadchanonaouz-toh.

Præter tense.

1 sing.

I wish I did pay thee,
Kuppapaumununaz-toh.
I wish I did pay him,
nuppapaumónaz-toh.
I wish I did pay you,
kuppapaumununnaouz-toh.

I wish I did pay them,
nuppapaumonaouz-toh.

2 sing.

I wish thou didst pay me,
Kuppapaumincaz-toh.
I wish thou didst pay him,
kuppapaumonaz-toh.
I wish thou didst pay us,
kuppapaumuncanonuz-toh.

I wish thou didst pay them,
kuppapaumónaouz-toh.

3 sing.

I wish he did pay me,
Nuppapaumukqunaz-toh.
I wish he did pay thee,
kuppapaumukqunaz-toh.
I wish he did pay him,
uppapaumónaz-toh.
I wish he did pay us,
nuppapaumukqunanonuz-
toh.
I wish he did pay you,
kuppapaumukqunaouz-toh.

I wish he did pay them,
uppapaumonaouz-toh.

Optative Mode.

Præter tense.

1 plur.

I wish we did keep thee,
Kœwaadchanònanonuz-
toh.
I wish we did keep him,
nœwaadchanònanonuz-toh.
I wish we did keep you,
kœwaadchanunanònaz-toh.
I wish we did keep them,
nœwaadchanonanonuz-toh.

2 plur.

I wish ye did keep me,
Kœwaadchanincaouz-toh.
I wish ye did keep him,
kœwaadchanonaòuz-toh.
I wish ye did keep us,
kœwaadchaninncanonuz-
toh.
I wish ye did keep them,
kœwaadchanónaouz-toh.

3 plur.

I wish they did keep me,
Nœwaadchanukqunnaóuz-
toh.
I wish they did keep thee,
kœwaadchanukqunaóuz-
toh.
I wish they did keep him,
œwaadchanónaóuz-toh.
I wish they did keep us,
nœwaadchanukqunnanouz-
toh.
I wish they did keep you,
kœwaadchanukqunaòuz-
toh.
I wish they did keep them,
œwaadchanónaouz-toh.

Præter tense.

1 plur.

I wish we did pay thee,
Kuppapaumunanonuz-toh.
I wish we did pay him,
nuppapaumónanonuz-toh.
I wish we did pay you,
kuppapaumunanonuz-toh.
I wish we did pay them,
nuppapaumonanonuz-toh.

2 plur.

I wish ye did pay me,
Kuppapaumincaouz-toh.
I wish ye did pay him,
kuppapaumonaouz-toh.
I wish ye did pay us,
kuppapaumincanonuz-toh.
I wish ye did pay them,
kuppapaumonaouz-toh.

3 plur.

I wish they did pay me,
Nuppapaumukqunaouz-toh.
I wish they did pay thee,
kuppapaumukqunaóuz-toh.
I wish they did pay him,
uppapaumónaòuz-toh.
I wish they did pay us,
nuppapaumukqunanonuz-
toh.
I wish they did pay you,
kuppapaumukqunaòuz-toh.
I wish they did pay them,
uppapaumónaouz-toh.

The *Suppositive Mode* of the *Suffix form animate Affirmative.*

Note, That this Mode also doth cast off the Affix, or prefixed Pronoun.

Present tense.	*Present tense.*

1 sing.
- *If I keep thee,* Wadchanunon.
- *If I keep him,* wadchanog.
- *If I keep you,* wadchanunóg.
- *If I keep them,* wadchaog.

1 sing.
- *If I pay thee,* Paumunon.
- *If I pay him,* paumog.
- *If I pay you,* paumunóg.
- *If I pay them,* paumog.

2 sing.
- *If thou keep me,*, Wadchanean.
- *If thou keep him,* wadchanadt.
- *If thou keep us,* wadchaneog.
- *If thou keep them,* wadchanadt.

2 sing.
- *If thou pay me,* Paumean.
- *If thou pay him,* paumadt.
- *If thou pay us,* paumeog.
- *If thou pay them,* paumadt.

3 sing.
- *If he keep me,* Wadchanit.
- *If he keep thee,* wadchanukquean.
- *If he keep him,* wadchanont.
- *If he keep us,* wadchanukqueog.
- *If he keep you,* wadchanukqueóg.
- *If he keep them,* wadchanûhettit, *or* ont.

3 sing.
- *If he pay me,* Paumit.
- *If he pay thee,* paumukquean.
- *If he pay him,* paumont.
- *If he pay us,* paumukqueog.
- *If he pay you,* paumukqueóg.
- *If he pay them,* paumûhettit.

Suppositíve Mode.

Note, *Where the singular and plural are alike, they are distinguished by* Noh *or* Neen *in the singular, and* Nag *or* Nenawun *in the plural.*

Present tense.

1 plur.
- *If we keep thee,*
Wadchanunog.
- *If we keep him,*
wadchanogkut.
- *If we keep you,*
wadchanunog.
- *If we keep them,*
wadchanogkut.

2 plur.
- *If ye keep me,*
Wadchancóg.
- *If ye keep him,*
wadchanóg.
- *If ye keep us,*
wadchancog.
- *If ye keep them,*
wadchanóg.

3 plur.
- *If they keep me,*
Wadchanhettit.
- *If they keep thee,*
wadchanukquean.
- *If they keep him,*
wadchanukáhettit.
- *If they keep us,*
wadchanukqueog.
- *If they keep you,*
wadchanukqueòg.
- *If they keep them,*
wadchanáhettit.

Present tense.

1 plur.
- *If we pay thee,*
Paumunog.
- *If we pay him,*
paumogkut.
- *If we pay you,*
paumunog.
- *If we pay them,*
paumogkut.

2 plur.
- *If ye pay me,*
Paumcóg.
- *If ye pay him,*
paumóg.
- *If ye pay us,*
paumcóg.
- *If ye pay them,*
paumóg.

3 plur.
- *If they pay me,*
Paumhettit.
- *If they pay thee,*
paumukquean.
- *If they pay him,*
paumáhettit.
- *If they pay us,*
paumukqueog.
- *If they pay you,*
paumukqueòg.
- *If they pay them,*
paumáhettit.

Suppositive Mode.

Præter tense.   *Præter tense.*

1 sing.

If I did keep thee,
Wadchanunos.
If I did keep him,
waàdchanogkus.
If I did keep you,
wadchanunógkus.
If I did keep them,
wadchanogkus.

1 sing.

If I did pay thee,
Paumunos.
If I did pay him,
paumogkus.
If I did pay you,
paumunógkus.
If I did pay them,
paumogkus.

2 sing.

If thou didst keep me,
Wadchaneas.
If thou didst keep him,
wadchanas.
If thou didst keep us,
wadchancogkus.
If thou didst keep them,
wadchanas.

2 sing.

If thou didst pay me,
Paumeas.
If thou didst pay him,
paumas.
If thou didst pay us,
paumeogkus.
If thou didst pay them,
paumas.

3 sing.

If he did keep me,
Wadchanis.
If he did keep thee,
wadchanukqueas.
If he did keep him,
wadchanós.
If he did keep us,
wadchanukqueogkus.
If he did keep you,
wadchanukqueógkus.
If he did keep them,
wadchanos.

3 sing.

If he did pay me,
Paumis.
If he did pay thee,
paumukqueas.
If he did pay him,
paumos.
If he did pay us,
paumukqueogkus.
If he did pay you,
paumukqueógkus.
If he did pay them,
paumos.

Suppositive Mode.

Præter tense.   *Præter tense.*

1 plur.
{
If we did keep thee,
wadchanunogkus.
If we did keep him,
wadchanogkutus.
If we did keep you,
wadchanunogkus.
If we did keep them,
wadchanogkutus.
}

1 plur.
{
If we did pay thee,
Paumunogkus.
If we did pay him,
paumunogkutus.
If we did pay you,
paumunogkus.
If we did pay them,
paumogkutus.
}

2 plur.
{
If ye did keep me,
Wadchaneógkus.
If ye did keep him,
wadchanógkus.
If ye did keep us,
wadchaneogkus.
If ye did keep them,
wadchanógkus.
}

2 plur.
{
If ye did pay me,
Paumeogkus.
If ye did pay him,
paumogkus.
If ye did pay us,
paumeogkus.
If ye did pay them,
paumógkus.
}

3 plur.
{
If they did keep me,
wadchanhettis.
If they did keep thee,
wadchanukqueas.
If they did keep him,
wadchanahettis.
If they did keep us,
wadchanukqueogkus.
If they did keep you,
wadchanukqueógkus.
If they did keep them,
wadchanahettis.
}

3 plur.
{
If they did pay me,
Paumehettis.
If they did pay thee,
paumukqueas.
If they did pay him,
paumahettis.
If they did pay us,
paumukqueogkus.
· If they did pay you,
paumukqueógkus.
If they did pay them,
paumahettis.
}

[p. 42.]

The Indefinite Mode.

Present tense.

To keep,
Wadchanónat.

Present tense.

To pay,
Paummuonat.

The *third Person* of the *Suffix form Animate* is capable to be expressed in the *Indefinite Mode.*

Note also, *That this mode followeth the* Indicative *and keepeth the Affix.*

As for Example.

3 sing.
{
To keep me,
Nꝏwadchanukqunat.
To keep thee,
kꝏwadchanukqunat.
To keep him,
ꝏwadchanonat.
To keep us,
nꝏwadchanukqunnanonut.
To keep you,
kꝏwadchanukqunnaout.
To keep them,
ꝏwadchanonaout.
}

3 sing.
{
To pay me,
Nuppaumunkqunat.
To pay thee,
kuppaumukqunat.
To pay him,
uppaumonat.
To pay us,
nuppaumukqunnanonut.
To pay you,
kuppaumukqunnaout.
To pay them,
uppaumonaoont.
}

So much for the Suffix form Animate Affirmative.

[A blank page follows, in the original, between this page and 44.   Ed.]

10

The *Suffix form Animate* Negative.

Indicative Mode.

Present tense.

1 sing.
> I keep not thee,
> Kꝏwadchanunꝏh.
> I keep not him,
> nꝏwadchanòh.
> I keep not you,
> kꝏwadchanoog.
> I keep not them,
> Mat nꝏwadchanoog.

2 sing.
> Thou keep not me,
> Kꝏwadchaneûh.
> Thou keep not him,
> kꝏwadchanòh.
> Thou keep not us,
> kꝏwadchaneumun.
> Thou keep not them,
> Mat kꝏwadchanoog.

3 sing.
> He keep not me,
> Nꝏwadchanukꝏh.
> He keep not thee,
> kꝏwadchanukꝏh.
> He keep not him,
> Mat ꝏwadchanuh.
> He keep not us,
> nꝏwadchanukꝏun.
> He keep not you,
> Mat kꝏwadchanukꝏ.
> He keep not them,
> Mat ꝏwadchanuh.

Present tense.

1 sing.
> I pay not thee,
> Kuppaumunꝏh.
> I pay not him,
> nuppaumòh.
> I pay not you,
> kuppaumunꝏmwꝏ.
> I pay not them,
> Mat nuppaumoog.

2 sing.
> Thou pay not me,
> Kuppaumeuh.
> Thou pay not him,
> kuppaumòh.
> Thou pay not us,
> kuppaumeumun.
> Thou pay not them,
> Mat kuppaumeumoog.

3 sing.
> He pay not me,
> Nuppaumukꝏh.
> He pay not thee,
> Kuppaumukꝏh.
> He pay not him,
> Mat uppaumoh.
> He pay not us,
> nuppaumukꝏun.
> He pay not you,
> Mat kuppaumukꝏh.
> He pay not them,
> Mat uppaumuh.

Indicative Mode.

Present tense.

Present tense.

1 plur.
- We keep not thee,
  Kꝏwadchanunꝏmun.
- We keep not him,
  mat nꝏwadchanóun.
- We keep not you,
  kꝏwadchanunꝏmun.
- We keep not them,
  mat nꝏwadchanounonog.

1 plur.
- We pay not thee,
  Kuppaumvnꝏmun.
- We pay not him,
  mat nuppaumoun.
- We pay not you,
  kuppaumunꝏmun.
- We pay not them,
  mat nuppaumounonog.

2 plur.
- Ye keep not me,
  Kꝏwadchaneumwꝏ.
- Ye keep not him,
  mat kꝏwadchanau.
- Ye keep not us,
  kꝏwadchaneumun.
- Ye keep not them,
  mat kꝏwadchanoog.

2 plur.
- Ye pay not me,
  Kuppaumeumwꝏ.
- Ye pay not him,
  mat kuppaumau.
- Ye pay not us,
  kuppaumeumun.
- Ye pay not them,
  mat kuppaumoog.

3 plur.
- They keep not me,
  Nꝏwadchanukꝏog.
- They keep not thee,
  kꝏwadchanukꝏog.
- They keep not him,
  mat ꝏwadchanouh.
- They keep not us,
  nꝏwadchanukꝏunonog.
- They keep not you,
  kꝏwadchanukꝏoog.
- They keep not them,
  mat ꝏwadchanouh.

3 plur.
- They pay not me,
  Nuppaumukꝏog.
- They pay not thee,
  kuppaumukꝏog.
- They pay not him,
  mat uppaumouh.
- They pay not us,
  nuppaumukꝏunonog.
- They pay not you,
  kuppaumukꝏoog.
- They pay not them,
  mat uppaumouh.

Indicative Mode.

Præter tense.

1 sing. {
  I did not keep thee,
  Kꝏwadchanunꝏp.
  I did not keep him,
  mat nꝏwadchanóhp.
  I did not keep you,
  kꝏwadchanunꝏmwop.
  I did not keep them,
  mat nꝏwadchanopanneg.

2 sing. {
  Thou didst not keep me,
  Kꝏwadchaneup.
  Thou didst not keep him,
  mat kꝏwadchanóp.
  Thou didst not keep us,
  kꝏwadchaneumunonup.
  Thou didst not keep them,
  mat kꝏwadchanopanneg.

3 sing. {
  He did not keep me,
  Nꝏwadchanukꝏp.
  He did not keep thee,
  kꝏwadchanukꝏp.
  He did not keep him,
  mat ꝏwadchanópoh.
  He did not keep us,
  nꝏwadchanukꝏunonup.
  He did not keep you,
  kꝏwadchanukꝏp.
  He did not keep them,
  mat ꝏwadchanopoh.

Præter tense.

1 sing. {
  I did not pay thee,
  Kuppaumunꝏp.
  I did not pay him,
  mat nuppaumóp.
  I did not pay you,
  kuppaumunꝏmwop.
  I did not pay them,
  mat nuppaumopanneg.

2 sing. {
  Thou didst not pay me,
  Kuppaumeup.
  Thou didst not pay him,
  mat kuppaumòp.
  Thou didst not pay us,
  kuppaumeumunònup.
  Thou didst not pay them,
  mat kuppaumopanneg.

3 sing. {
  He did not pay me,
  Nuppaumukꝏp.
  He did not pay thee,
  kuppaumukꝏp.
  He did not pay him,
  mat paumópoh.
  He did not pay us,
  nuppaumukꝏunonup.
  He did not pay you,
  kuppaumukꝏp.
  He did not pay them,
  mat uppaumopoh.

Indicative Mode.

Præter tense.   *Præter tense.*

1 *plur.*
{
We did not keep thee,
Kꝏwadchaninꝏmunonup.
We did not keep him,
mat nꝏwadchanounonup.
We did not keep you,
kꝏwadchaninꝏmunonup.
We did not keep them,
mat nꝏwadchanounonup-
   panneg.
}

1 *plur.*
{
We did not pay thee,
Kuppaumunꝏmunonup.
We did not pay him,
mat nuppaumounonup.
We did not pay you,
kuppaumunꝏmunonup.
We did not pay them,
mat nuppaumounonup-
   paneg.
}

2 *plur.*
{
Ye did not keep me,
Kꝏwadchaneumwop.
Ye did not keep him,
mat kꝏwadchanꝏop.
Ye did not keep us,
kꝏwadchaneumunonup.
Ye did not keep them,
mat kꝏwadchanoopanneg.
}

2 *plur.*
{
Ye did not pay me,
Kuppaumeumwop.
Ye did not pay him,
mat kuppaumꝏop.
Ye did not pay us,
kuppaumeumunonup.
. Ye did not pay them,
mat kuppaumꝏopanneg.
}

3 *plur.*
{
They did not keep me,
Nꝏwadchanukꝏpanneg.
They did not keep thee,
kꝏwadchanukꝏpanneg.
They did not keep him,
mat ꝏwadchanꝏopoh.
They did not keep us,
nꝏwadchanukꝏunonup-
   panneg.
They did not keep you,
kꝏwadchanukꝏoopanneg.
They did not keep them,
mat ꝏwadchanꝏopoh.
}

3 *plur.*
{
They did not pay me,
Nuppaumukꝏpanneg.
They did not pay thee,
kuppaumukꝏpanneg.
They did not pay him,
mat uppaumꝏopuh.
They did not pay us,
nuppaumukꝏunonuppau-
   neg.
They did not pay you,
kuppaumukꝏoopanneg.
They did not pay them,
mat uppaumꝏopoh.
}

The *Suffix form animate* Negative.

Imperative Mode.

Present tense.

1 sing.
- Let me not keep thee, Wadchanunꝏutti.
- Let me not keep him, wadchanoonti.
- Let me not keep you, wadchanunonkqutti.
- Let me not keep them, wadchanoonti.

2 sing.
- Do thou not keep me, Wadchanohkon.
- Do thou not keep him, wadchanuhkon.
- Do thou not keep us, wadchanéittuh.
- Do thou not keep them, wadchanuhkon.

3 sing.
- Let not him keep me, Wadchanehkitch.
- Let not him keep thee, wadchanukꝏhkon.
- Let not him keep him, wadchanuhkitch.
- Let not him keep us, wadchanukꝏuttuh.
- Let not him keep you, wadchanukꝏhteók.
- Let not him keep them, wadchanuhkitch.

Present tense.

1 sing.
- Let me not pay thee, Paumunutti.
- Let me not pay him, paumoonti.
- Let me not pay you, paumunꝏutti.
- Let me not pay them, paumoonti.

2 sing.
- Do thou not pay me, Paumchkon.
- Do thou not pay him, paumuhkon.
- Do thou not pay us, pauméittuh.
- Do thou not pay them, paumóhkon.

3 sing.
- Let not him pay me, Paumehkitch.
- Let not him pay thee, paumukꝏhkon.
- Let not him pay him, paumuhkitch.
- Let not him pay us, paumukꝏuttuh.
- Let not him pay you, paumukꝏhteók.
- Let not him pay them, paumuhkitch.

Imperative Mode.

Present tense.

Present tense.

1 plur.
> *Let not us keep thee,*
> Wadchanunꝏuttuh.
> *Let not us keep him,*
> wadchanóontuh.
> *Let not us keep you,*
> wadchanunꝏuttuh.
> *Let not us keep them,*
> wadchanoortuh.

2 plur.
> *Do not ye keep me,*
> Wadchanehteók.
> *Do not ye keep him,*
> wadchanuhteók.
> *Do not ye keep us,*
> wadchanéinnean.
> *Do not ye keep them,*
> wadchanuhteók.

3 plur.
> *Let not them keep me,*
> Wadchanehettekitch.
> *Let not them keep thee,*
> wadchanukꝏhkon.
> *Let not them keep him,*
> wadchanahettekitch.
> *Let not them keep us,*
> wadchanukꝏuttuh.
> *Let not them keep you,*
> wadchanukꝏhteok.
> *Let not them keep them,*
> wadchanahettekitch.

1 plur.
> *Let not us pay thee,*
> Paumunꝏuttuh.
> *Let not us pay him,*
> paumoontuh.
> *Let not us pay you,*
> paumunꝏuttuh.
> *Let not us pay them,*
> paumoontuh.

2 plur.
> *Do not ye pay me,*
> Paumehteok.
> *Do not ye pay him,*
> paumuhteok.
> *Do not ye pay us,*
> pauméinnean.
> *Do not ye pay them,*
> paumuhteok.

3 plur.
> *Let not them pay me,*
> Paumehettekitch.
> *Let not them pay thee,*
> paumukꝏhkon.
> *Let not them pay him,*
> paumahettekitch.
> *Let not them pay us,*
> paumukꝏuttuh.
> *Let not them pay you,*
> paumukꝏhteok.
> *Let not them pay them,*
> paumahettekitch.

The *Suffix form Animate* Negative.

Optative Mode.

Present tense.

1 sing.

I wish I keep not thee,
Koowaadchanunooun-toh.
I wish I keep not him,
noowaadchanoun-toh.
I wish I keep not you,
koowaadchanunoouneau-toh
I wish I keep not them,
noowaadchanouneau-toh.

2 sing.

I wish thou do not keep me,
Koowaadchancin-toh.
I wish thou do not keep him
koowaadchanoon-toh.
I wish thou do not keep us,
koowaadchancin-toh.
I wish thou do not keep them
koowaadchanouneau-toh.

3 sing.

I wish he do not keep me,
Noowaadchanukooun-toh.
I wish he do not keep thee,
koowaadchanukooun-toh.
I wish he do not keep him,
oowaadchanoon-toh.
I wish he do not keep us,
noowaadchanukoounan-toh.
I wish he do not keep you,
koowaadchanukoouneau-toh
I wish he do not keep them,
oowaadchanoon-toh.

Present tense.

1 sing.

I wish I do not pay t
Kuppapaumunooun-toh
I wish I do not pay l
nuppapaumoon-toh.
I wish I do not pay y
kuppapaumunoouneau-
I wish I do not pay t
nuppapaumouneau-toh

2 sing.

I wish thou do not pa
Kuppapauméin-toh.
I wish thou do not pay
kuppapaumoon-toh.
I wish thou do not p
kuppapauméinan-toh.
I wish thou do not pay
kuppapaumouneau-tol

3 sing.

I wish he do not pay
Nuppapaumukooun-tol
I wish he do not pay
kuppapaumukooun-toh
I wish he do not pay
uppapaumoun-toh.
I wish he do not pay
nuppapaumukoounan-t
I wish he do not pay
kuppapaumukoouneau
I wish he do not pay
uppapaumouneau-toh.

Optative Mode.

Present tense.

1 plur.
> *I wish we do not keep thee,*
> Kꝏwaadchanunꝏunan-toh.
> *I wish we do not keep him,*
> nꝏwaadchanounan-toh.
> *I wish we do not keep you,*
> kꝏwaadchanounan-toh.
> *I wish we do not keep them*
> nꝏwaadchanounan-toh.

2 plur.
> *I wish ye do not keep me,*
> Kꝏwaadchaneinneau-toh.
> *I wish ye do not keep him,*
> kꝏwaadchanouneau-toh.
> *I wish ye do not keep us,*
> kꝏwaadchanéinnean-toh.
> *I wish ye do not keep them,*
> kꝏwaadchanouneau-toh.

3 plur.
> *I wish they do not keep me,*
> Nꝏwaadchanukꝏuneau-toh.
> *I wish they do not keep thee,*
> kꝏwaadchanukꝏuneau-toh
> *I wish they do not keep him,*
> ꝏwaadchanouneau-toh.
> *I wish they do not keep us,*
> nꝏwaadchanukꝏunan-toh.
> *I wish they do not keep you,*
> kꝏwaadchanukꝏuneau-toh
> *I wish they do not keep them,*
> ꝏwaadchanouneau-toh.

Present tense.

1 plur.
> *I wish we do not pay thee,*
> Kuppapaumunꝏon-toh.
> *I wish we do not pay him,*
> nuppapaumoon-toh.
> *I wish we do not pay you,*
> kuppapaumunꝏunan-toh.
> *I wish we do not pay them,*
> nuppapaumounan-toh.

2 plur.
> *I wish ye do not pay me,*
> Kuppapauméineau-toh.
> *I wish ye do not pay him,*
> kuppapaumooneau-toh.
> *I wish ye do not pay us,*
> kuppapauméinan-toh.
> *I wish ye do not pay them,*
> kuppapaumooneau-toh.

3 plur.
> *I wish they do not pay me,*
> Nuppapaumukꝏuneau-toh.
> *I wish they do not pay thee,*
> kuppapaumukꝏuneau-toh.
> *I wish they do not pay him,*
> uppapaumouneau-toh.
> *I wish they do not pay us,*
> nuppapaumukꝏunan-toh.
> *I wish they do not pay you,*
> kuppapaumukꝏuneau-toh.
> *I wish they do not pay them,*
> uppapaumouneau-toh.

11

Optative Mode.

Præter tense.   *Præter tense.*

1 sing.
I wish I did not keep thee,
Kꝏwaadchanunꝏunaz-toh.
I wish I did not keep him,
nꝏwaadchanòunaz-toh.
I wish I did not keep you,
kꝏwaadchanunoũnaouz-
toh.
I wish I did not keep them,
nꝏwaadchanòunaouz-toh.

1 sing.
I wish I did not pay thee,
Kuppapaumunꝏunaz-toh.
I wish I did not pay him,
nuppapaủmounaz-toh.
I wish I did not pay you,
kuppapaumunꝏunaouz-toh
I wish I did not pay them,
nuppapaumounaouz-toh.

2 sing.
I wish thou didst not keep me,
Kꝏwaadchanéinaz-toh.
I wish thou didst not keep him,
kꝏwaadchanóunaz-toh.
I wish thou didst not keep us,
kꝏwaadchaneinanonaz-toh
I wish thou didst not keep
them,
kꝏwaadchanounnaouz-toh.

2 sing.
I wish thou didst not pay me
Kuppapauméinaz-toh.
I wish thou didst not pay him
kuppapaumounaz-toh.
I wish thou didst not pay us
kuppapauméinanonuz-toh.
I wish thou didst not pay them
kuppapaumounaouz-toh.

3 sing.
I wish he did not keep me,
Nꝏwaadchanukꝏunaz-toh.
I wish he did not keep thee,
kꝏwaadchanukꝏunaz-toh.
I wish he did not keep him,
ꝏwaadchanounaz-toh.
I wish he did not keep us,
nꝏwaadchanukꝏunanon-
uz-toh.
I wish he did not keep you,
kꝏwaadchanukꝏaunouz-
toh.
I wish he did not keep them,
ꝏwaadchanòunaouz-toh.

3 sing.
I wish he did not pay me,
Nuppapaumulkꝏunaz-toh.
I wish he did not pay thee,
kuppapaumukꝏunaz-toh.
I wish he did not pay him,
uppapaumóunaz-toh.
I wish he did not pay us,
nuppapaumukꝏñanonuz-
toh.
I wish he did not pay you,
kuppapaumukꝏunaouz-to
I wish he did not pay them,
uppapaumounaz-toh.

Optative Mode.

Præter tense.	*Præter tense.*

1 plur.

I wish we did not keep thee,
Koowaadchanunꝏunanonuz-toh.
I wish we did not keep him,
nꝏwaadchanòunanouz-toh.
I wish we did not keep you,
koowaadchanꝏunaouz-toh.
I wish we did not keep them,
nꝏwaadchanꝏunaouz-toh.

1 plur.

I wish we did not pay thee,
Kuppapaumunꝏunanonuz-toh.
I wish we did not pay him,
nuppapaumounanonuz-toh.
I wish we did not pay you,
kuppapaumunꝏunaoaz-toh
I wish we did not pay them,
nuppapaumounaóaz-toh.

2 plur.

I wish ye did not keep me,
Koowaadchanéinaòuz-toh.
I wish ye did not keep him,
koowaadchanónuaouz-toh.
I wish ye did not keep us,
koowaadchanéinanonaz-toh
I wish ye did not keep them,
koowaadchanounaouz-toh.

2 plur.

I wish ye did not pay me,
Kuppapauméinaoaz-toh.
I wish ye did not pay him,
kuppapaumoonaoaz-toh.
I wish ye did not pay us,
kuppapauméinnanonaz-toh
I wish ye did not pay them,
kuppapaumoonaoaz-toh.

3 plur.

I wish they did not keep me,
Nꝏwaadchanukꝏunaz-toh.
I wish they did not keep thee,
koowaadchanukꝏunaz-toh.
I wish they did not keep him,
ꝏwaadchanounaoaz-toh.
I wish they did not keep us,
nꝏwaadchanukꝏunanonaz-toh.
I wish they did not keep you,
koowaadchanukꝏunaouz-toh.
I wish they did not keep them,
ꝏwaadchanounaoaz-toh.

3 plur.

I wish they did not pay me,
Nuppapaumukꝏunaooz-toh.
I wish they did not pay thee,
kuppapaumukꝏunaooz-toh
I wish they did not pay him,
uppapaumoonaz-toh.
I wish they did not pay us,
nuppapaumukꝏnnuanonaz-toh.
I wish they did not pay you,
kuppapaumukꝏunaoaz-toh
I wish they did not pay them,
uppapaumounaoaz-toh.

The *Suffix form Animate* Negative.

Suppositive Mode.

Present tense.   *Present tense.*

1 sing.
- If *I keep not thee,* Wadchanunᴏᴏon.
- If *I keep not him,* wadchanoog.
- If *I keep not you,* wadchanunᴏᴏog.
- If *I keep not them,* wadchanoog.

1 sing.
- If *I pay not thee,* Paumunᴏᴏon.
- If *I pay not him,* Paumoog.
- If *I pay not you,* Paumunᴏᴏóg.
- If *I pay not them,* Paumoog.

2 sing.
- If *thou keep not me,* wadchaneean.
- If *thou keep not him,* wadchanoadt.
- If *thou keep not us,* wadchaneeog.
- If *thou keep not them,* wadchanoadt.

2 sing.
- If *thou pay not me,* Paumeean.
- If *thou pay not him,* Paumoadt.
- If *thou pay not us,* Paumeeog.
- If *thou pay not them,* Paumoadt.

3 sing.
- If *he keep not me,* Wadchaneegk.
- If *he keep not thee,* wadchanukᴏᴏan.
- If *he keep not him,* wadchanunk.
- If *he keep not us,* wadchanukᴏᴏog.
- If *he keep not you,* wadchanukᴏᴏóg.
- If *he keep not them,* wadchanunk.

3 sing.
- If *he pay not me,* Paumeegk.
- If *he pay not thee,* paumukᴏᴏan.
- If *he pay not him,* paum'unk.
- If *he pay not us,* paumukᴏᴏog.
- If *he pay not you,* paumukᴏᴏóg.
- If *he pay not them,* paumunk.

Suppositive Mode.

Present tense.   *Present tense.*

1 plur.
- *If we keep not thee,* Wadchanunꝏog.
- *If we keep not him,* wadchanoogkut.
- *If we keep not you,* wadchanunꝏog.
- *If we keep not them,* wadchanoogkut.

2 plur.
- *If ye keep not me,* Wadchaneeóg.
- *If ye keep not him,* wadchanoóg.
- *If ye keep not us,* wadchaneeog.
- *If ye keep not them,* wadchanoóg.

3 plur.
- *If they keep not me,* Wadchanehetteg.
- *If they keep not thee,* wadchanukꝏan.
- *If they keep not him,* wadchanahetteg.
- *If they keep not us,* wadchanukꝏog.
- *If they keep not you,* wadchanukꝏóg.
- *If they keep not them,* wadchanahetteg.

1 plur.
- *If we pay not thee,* Paumunꝏog.
- *If we pay not him,* paumoogkut.
- *If we pay not you,* paumunꝏóg.
- *If we pay not them,* paumoogkut.

2 plur.
- *If ye pay not me,* Paumeeòg.
- *If ye pay not him,* paumôòg.
- *If ye pay not us,* paumeeog.
- *If ye pay not them,* paumôòg.

3 plur.
- *If they pay not me,* Paumehetteg.
- *If they pay not thee,* paumukꝏan.
- *If they pay not him,* paumahetteg.
- *If they pay not us,* paumukꝏog.
- *If they pay not you,* paumukꝏog.
- *If they pay not them,* paumahetteg.

Suppositive Mode.

Præter tense.   *Præter tense.*

1 sing.
{ *If I did not keep thee,*
Wadchanunꝏos.
If I did not keep him,
wadchanoogkus.
If I did not keep you,
wadchanunꝏógkus.
If I did not keep them,
wadchanoogkus.

1 sing.
{ *If I did not pay thee,*
Paumunꝏos.
If I did not pay him,
paumoogkus.
If I did not pay you,
paumunꝏógkus.
If I did not pay them
paumoogkus.

2 sing.
{ *If thou didst not keep me,*
Wadchanceas.
If thou didst not keep him,
wadchanoas.
If thou didst not keep us,
wadchanceogkus.
If thou didst not keep them,
wadchanoógkus.

2 sing.
{ *If thou didst not pay*
Paumceas.
If thou didst not pay
paumoas.
If thou didst not pay
paumceogkus.
If thou didst not pay
paumoógkus.

3 sing.
{ *If he did not keep me,*
Wadchancekus.
If he did not keep thee,
wadchanukꝏas.
If he did not keep him,
wadchanunkus.
If he did not keep us,
wadchanukꝏꝏógkus.
If he did not keep you,
wadchanukógkus.
If he did not keep them,
wadchanunkus.

3 sing.
{ *If he did not pay me*
Paumeekus.
If he did not pay the
paumukꝏas.
If he did not pay hi
paumunkus.
If he did not pay us
paumukꝏoogkus.
If he did not pay yo
paumukꝏógkus.
If he did not pay th
paumunkus.

Suppositive Mode.

Præter tense.   *Præter tense.*

1 plur.
If *we did not keep thee,*
Wadchanunꝏogkus.
If *we did not keep him,*
wadchanoogkutus.
If *we did not keep you,*
wadchanunꝏógkus.
If *we did not keep them,*
wadchanoogkutus.

1 pur.
If *we did not pay thee,*
Paumunꝏogkus.
If *we did not pay him,*
paumoogkutus.
If *we did not pay you,*
paumunꝏógkus.
If *we did not pay them,*
paumoogkutus.

2 plur.
If *ye did not keep me,*
Wadchanecógkus.
If *ye did not keep him,*
wadchanoógkus.
If *ye did not keep us,*
wadchanecogkus.
If *ye did not keep them,*
wadchanoógkus.

2 plur.
If *ye did not pay me,*
Paumecógkus.
If *ye did not pay him,*
paumoógkus.
If *ye did not pay us,*
paumecogkus.
If *ye did not pay them,*
paumoógkus.

3 plur.
If *they did not keep me,*
Wadchanchettegkis.
If *they did not keep thee,*
wadchanukꝏas.
If *they did not keep him,*
wadchanunkus.
If *they did not keep us,*
wadchanukꝏogkus.
If *they did not keep you,*
wadchanukꝏógkus.
If *they did not keep them,*
wadchanahettegkis.

3 phur.
If *they did not pay me,*
Paumehcttegkis.
If *they did not pay thee,*
paumukꝏas.
If *they did not pay him,*
paumunkus.
If *they did not pay us,*
paumukꝏogkus.
If *they did not pay you,*
paumukꝏògkus.
If *they did not pay them,*
paumahcttegkis.

[p. 58.]

The Indefinite Mode.

Present tense.   *Present tense.*

Not to keep,   *Not to pay,*
Wadchanounat.   Paummuõunat.

The *third Person* of the *Suffix form Animate Nega*
is found expressible in this *Mode Indefinite :* As

3 *sing.*
{
Not to keep me,
Nꝏwadchanukꝏunat.
Not to keep thee,
kꝏwadchanukꝏunat.
Not to keep him,
ꝏwadchanounat.
Not to keep us,
nꝏwadchanukꝏunnanonut.
Not to keep you,
kꝏwadchanukꝏunnaout.
Not to keep them,
ꝏwadchanounat.

3 *sing.*
{
Not to pay me,
Nuppaumunkꝏunat.
Not to pay thee,
kuppaumukꝏunat.
Not to pay him,
uppaumounat.
Not to pay us,
nuppaumukꝏunnanon
Not to pay you,
kuppaumukꝏunnaout.
Not to pay them,
uppaumounnaout.

So much for the Suffix form Animate Negative.

The *Suffix form Animate Causative* is not universally applicable to this *Verb*; neither have I yet fully beat it out: onely in some chief wayes of the use of it in Speech I shall here set down, leaving the rest for afterwards, if God will, and that I live to adde unto this beginning.

Affirmative.	*Negative.*
1 { *I cause thee to keep me,* Koowadchanumwaheshnuh-hog. *I cause thee to keep him,* koowadchanumwahunun. *I cause thee to keep them,* koowadchanumwahunununk.	1 { *I cause thee not to keep me,* Koowadchanꭎwahꭎꭎhnuh-hog. *I cause thee not to keep him,* koowadchanumwahunꭎoun. *I cause thee not to keep them,* koowadchanumwahunꭎo-unꭎk.
2 { *Thou makest me keep him,* Koowadchanumwahen. *Thou makest me keep them,* koowadchanumwáheneunk.	2 { *Thou makest me not keep him,* Koowadchanumwahéin. *Thou makest me not keep them,* koowȧdchanumwaheinunk.
3 { *He maketh me keep him,* Noowadchanumwahikꭎun-uh. *He maketh me keep them,* nah noowadchanꭎwahik-qꭎuh.	3 { *He maketh me not keep him,* Noowadchanumwahikꭎoun-uh. *He maketh me not keep them,* Ibid.

Imperative Mode.

{ *Make me keep him,* Wadchanumwaheh n noh. *Make me keep them,* Nah wadchanumwaheh.	{ *Make me not keep him,* wadchanumwahehkon. *Make me not keep them,* Ibid.

Suppositive Mode.

{ *If thou make me keep him,* Wadchanumwahean ycuoh	{ *If thou make me not keep him,* Wadchanumwahccan.

12

[p. 60.]

I WAS purposed to put in no more Paradigms of Verbs; but considering that all Languages (so farre as I know) and this also, do often make use of the Verb Subtantive Passive, and in the reason of Speech it is of frequent use: Considering also that it doth differ in information from other Verbs, and that Verbals are often derived out of this form, as Wadchanittuonk, Salvation, &c. &c. I have therefore here put down an Example thereof.

The Verb Substantive Passive.

Nꝏwadchanit,   *I am kept.*

Indicative Mode.

Present tense.

sing. {
I am kept,
Nꝏwadchanit.
Thou art kept,
kꝏwadchanit.
He is kept,
wadchanau.
}

Present tense.

plur. {
We are kept,
Nꝏwadchanitteamun.
Ye are kept,
kꝏwadchanitteamwꝏ.
They are kept,
wadchanoog.
}

Præter tense.

sing. {
I was kept,
Nꝏwadchanitteap.
Thou wast kept,
kꝏwadchanitteap.
He was kept,
wadchanop.
}

Præter tense.

plur. {
We were kept,
Nꝏwadchanitteamunónu
Ye were kept,
kꝏwadchanitteamwóp.
They were kept,
wadchanopanneg.
}

Imperative Mode.

sing.
{
Let me be kept,
Wadchanitteadti.
Be thou kept,
wadchanitteash.
Let him be kept,
wadchanaj.
}

plur.
{
Let us be kept,
Wadchanitteatuh.
Be ye kept,
wadchanitteak.
Let them be kept,
wadchanaj.
}

Optative Mode.

Present tense.

sing.
{
I wish I be kept,
Nꝏwaadchanittean-toh.
I wish thou be kept,
kꝏwaadchanittean-toh.
I wish he be kept,
waadchanon-toh.
}

Present tense.

plur.
{
I wish we be kept,
Nꝏwaadchanitteanan-toh.
I wish ye be kept,
kꝏwaadchanitteaneau-toh.
I wish they be kept,
waadchanoneau-toh.
}

Præter tense.

sing.
{
I wish I was kept,
Nꝏwaadchanitteanaz-toh.

I wish thou wast kept,
kꝏwaadchanitteanaz-toh.
I wish he was kept,
waadchanònaz-toh.
}

Præter tense.

plur.
{
I wish we were kept,
Nꝏwaadchanitteananònuz-toh.
I wish ye were kept,
kꝏwaadchanitteanaouz-toh
I wish they were kept,
waadchanonaouz-toh.
}

[p. 62.]

Suppositive Mode.

Present tense.

sing. { *When I am kept,*
Wadchanitteaon.
When thou art kept,
wadchanitteaan.
When he is kept,
wadchanit noh.

Present tense.

plur. { *When we are kept,*
Wadchanitteaog.
When ye are kept,
wadchanitteaóg.
When they are kept,
wadchanit nag.

The *Præter tense* is formed by *adding* (us or ás) unto the *Present tense.*

Indefinite Mode.

Wadchanittéinât, · *To be kept.*

The form *Negative* of the Verb *Substantive Passive.*

Indicative Mode.

Present tense.

sing. { *I am not kept,*
Noowadchanitteòh.
Thou art not kept,
koowadchanitteòh.
He is not kept,
Mat wadchanau.

Present tense.

plur. { *We are not kept,*
Noowadchanitteoumun.
Ye are not kept,
koowadchanitteoumwoo.
They are not kept,
Mat wadchanoog.

Præter tense.

sing. { *I was not kept,*
Noowadchanitteohp.
Thou wast not kept,
koowadchanitteohp.
He was not kept,
Mat wadchanôuop.

Præter tense.

plur. { *We were not kept,* [up.
Noowadchanitteoumunnon-
Ye were not kept,
koowadchanitteoumwop.
They were not kept,
Mat wadchanoop.

Imperative Mode of the form *Negative Passive.*

sing. {
Be thou not kept,
Wadchanittuhkon.
Let not him be kept,
wadchittekitch.

plur. {
Be not ye kept,
Wadchanittuhkook.
Let not them be kept,
wadchanittekhettich.

Suppositive Mode Passive Negative.

Present tense.

Present tense.

sing. {
When I am not kept,
Wadchaneumuk.
When thou art not kept,
wadchaninomuk.
When he is not kept,
wadchanómuk.

{
The *Plural* is formed by *adding* (Mat) unto the form *Affirmative.*

The *Præter tense* is formed by *adding* [us or ás] to the *Present tense.*

The *Indefinite Mode Passive* Negative.

Wadchanóunát,   *Not to be kept.*

[p. 64.]

A TABLE of the Grammar of the *Suffix Verbs*
matical *Addition* after the word, are set down:
in the *Indicative* and *Optative Modes:* The *Imperc*
by the Suffix. Also note that (*I* him) and (*T*
the *Affix;* and (*Do thou*   him) in the *Imperc*
and what is prefixed or suffixed to the *Radi*

Indicative Mode.

Imperative Mode

Present tense.

1
1 oush
2 *radic.*
3 unumwoo
4 oog

2
1 eh *or* ah
2 *radic.*
3 imun
4 oog

3
1 uk
2 uk
3 oh *or* uh
4 ukqun
5 ukkou
6 oh *or* uh

1
1 unumun
2 óun
3 unumun
4 óunónog

2
1 imwoo
2 au
3 imun
4 auoog

3
1 ukquog
2 ukquog
3 ouh
4 ukqunonog
5 ukoooog
6 ouh

Præter tense.

1
1 unup
2 óp
3 unumwop
4 opanneg

2
1 ip
2 op
3 imunónup
4 opanneg

3
1 ukup
2 ukup
3 opoh
4 ukqunónup
5 ukoowop
6 opoh

1
1 unumunónup
2 óunónup
3 unumunónup
4 óunónuppanneg

2
1 imwop
2 auop
3 imunónup
4 auopanneg

3
1 ukuppanneg
2 ukuppanneg
3 auopuh   [neg
4 ukqunónuppan-
5 ukoóopanneg
6 auopoh

Imperative Mode

1
1 unutti
2 onti
3 unonkqutch
4 onti

2
1 eh
2 *radic.*
3 innean
4 *radic.*

3
1 itch
2 ukqush
3 onch
4 ukqutteuh
5 ukook
6 onch

1
1 unuttuh
2 ontuh
3 unuttuh
4 ontuh

2
1 egk *or* ig
2 ók
3 innean
4 ók

3
1 ukquttei *or*
2 ukqush[hett
3 ahettich
4 ukqutteuh
5 ukook
6 ahettich

firmative, wherein onely the *Suffixes*, viz. The Gram-
for the *Affix* or *Prefix*, you may observe it is used onely
and *Suppositive Modes* lay it by, and are varied onely
him) in the *Indicative Mode*, is the *Radicall word* with
Mode is the *Radicall word* without any *Affix* or *Suffix:*
Grammar.

Optative Mode.   Suppositive Mode.

Present tense.	Præter tense.	Present tense.	Præter tense.
1 { 1 unon / 2 on / 3 uneau / 4 óneau	1 { 1 unuaz / 2 ónaz / 3 ununnaóuz / 4 ónaóuz	1 { 1 unon / 2 og / 3 uncg / 4 òg	1 { 1 unos / 2 ogkus / 3 unogkus / 4 ogkus
2 { 1 in / 2 on / 3 unean / 4 óneau	2 { 1 incaz / 2 onaz / 3 uncanónuz / 4 ónaóuz	2 { 1 can / 2 adt *or* at / 3 cog / 4 adt *or* at	2 { 1 eas / 2 as / 3 egkus / 4 as
3 { 1 ukqun / 2 ukqun / 3 on / 4 ukqunán / 5 ukquneau / 6 on	3 { 1 ukqunaz / 2 ukqunaz / 3 onaz / 4 ukqunanonuz / 5 ukqunaóuz / 6 onaouz	3 { 1 it / 2 ukquean / 3 ont / 4 ukqueog / 5 ukqueóg / 6 ont	3 { 1 is / 2 ukqueas / 3 os / 4 ukqueogkus / 5 ukqueògkus / 6 os
1 { 1 unan / 2 ónán / 3 unan / 4 ónán	1 { 1 unanónuz / 2 ónanónuz / 3 unanónuz / 4 ónanonuz	1 { 1 unog / 2 ogkut / 3 unog / 4 ogkut	1 { 1 unogkus / 2 ogkutus / 3 unogkus / 4 ogkutus
2 { 1 uneau / 2 oneau / 3 unean / 4 óneau	2 { 1 ineaóuz / 2 ónaóuz / 3 ineanonuz / 4 ónaouz	2 { 1 eóg / 2 óg / 3 eóg / 4 òg	2 { 1 eógkus / 2 ògkus / 3 eógkus / 4 ogkus
3 { 1 ukquneau / 2 ukquneau / 3 óneau / 4 ukqunán / 5 ukquneau / 6 óneau	3 { 1 ukqunaouz / 2 ukqunaouz / 3 ónaouz / 4 ukqunanonuz / 5 ukqunaóuz / 6 ónaóuz	3 { 1 hettit / 2 ukquean / 3 úhettit / 4 ukqueog / 5 ukqueóg / 6 ahettit	3 { 1 ehettis / 2 ukqueas / 3 ahettis / 4 ukqueogkús / 5 ukqueòg / 6 ahettis

Onely remember that (toh) *is to
be annexed to every person
and variation in this Mode.*

[p. 66.]

I HAVE now finished what I shall do at present: and
a word or two to satisfie the prudent Enquirer how I fou
out these new wayes of Grammar, which no other Learn
Language (so far as I know) useth; I thus inform hir
God first put into my heart a compassion over their po
Souls, and a desire to teach them to know Christ, and to bri
them into his Kingdome. *Then presently I found out (*
God's wise providence) a pregnant witted young man, w
had been a *Servant in an English house, who pretty well u*
derstood his own Language, and hath a clear pronunciatio.
Him I made my Interpreter. *By his help I translated t*
Commandments, *the* Lord's Prayer, and *many* Texts
Scripture: *Also I compiled both* Exhortations *and* Praye
by his help. I *diligently marked* the difference of th
Grammar *from* ours: When I *found the way of them*
would pursue a word, *a* noun, *a* verb, *through all* var
tions *I could think of. And thus I came at it. We m*
not sit still and look for miracles; Up, and be doing, a
the Lord will be with thee. Prayer *and* pains, *throu*
faith in Christ Jesus will do any thing. Nil tam defic
quod non——I *do* believe *and* hope *that the Gospel sh*
be spread to all the ends of the Earth, and dark corners
the world by such a way, *and that such* Instruments *as t*
Churches *shall send forth for that end and purpose.* Lo
hasten those good days, and pour out that good Spirit up
thy people. Amen.

FINIS.

NOTES AND OBSERVATIONS ON ELIOT'S INDIAN GRAMMAR. ADDRESSED TO JOHN PICKERING, ESQ. BY PETER S. DU PONCEAU.*

THE great and good man, whose work has given rise to the following observations, did not foresee, when he wrote his Indian Grammar, that it would be sought after and studied by the learned of all nations, as a powerful help towards the improvement of a science not then in existence; I mean the *Comparative Science of Languages*, which of late has made such progress in our own country, as well as in *Europe* where our aboriginal idioms have become a subject of eager investigation. The *Augustine* of New England had no object in view, but that which he expresses in his title page—" the help of such as desired to learn the Indian language for the furtherance of the Gospel among the natives." But that worldly fame, which he did not seek, awaited him at the end of two centuries; and his works, though devoted to religion alone, have become important sources of human learning.

Religion and Science, well understood, are handmaids to each other. In no instance is this truth more evident than in the branch of knowledge of which we are treating. For it is to the unwearied and truly apostolick labours of Christian missionaries, and of societies instituted for the propagation of the Gospel among distant nations, that we are indebted for the immense materials which we already possess on the subject of the various languages of the earth. The Roman Congregation *De propagandâ fide* † gave the first impulse, which the zeal of the other Christian denominations has, in later times, not only followed but improved upon. The numerous translations of the sacred volume, which have been made under the patronage of the British, Russian, and American Bible Societies, into langua-

---

* These Remarks having been written at the suggestion of my learned friend, Mr. *Pickering*, I have thought it right to inscribe them to him as a just tribute of friendship and respect. P. S. D.

† Many Grammars, Dictionaries and Vocabularies of Asiatick, African and American languages, have been published under the direction of that Society, the only complete collection of which, perhaps, is in the Vatican or in their own library. As the science advances, they will no doubt be reprinted, as the present work is, for the benefit of the learned.

13

ges, many of which were till then unknown, except by th
names, have afforded ample means of comparison betwe
those various idioms ; the value of which is not yet so fu
understood, as there can be no doubt it will be at a future da

The object of this science is the study of man through th
noble faculty, which distinguishes him from the rest of the a
mal creation ; the faculty of " holding communication from s
to soul ;" an earnest, as I might say, and a foretaste of the
joyments of celestial life. It is a branch, and an importa
one, of the " history of the human mind ;" a subject, to
study of which the Lockes, the Mallebranches, the Reids,
Stewarts, the Wolfs, the Leibnitzs and other distinguished m
whose names it is needless to mention here, have devoted th
lives. The ignorant, it is true, have said that " metaphysi
is vanity ;" but the ignorant may jest as much as they w
they can never succeed in eradicating from the breast of
mortal man

> " This pleasing hope, this fond desire,
> This longing after something unpossess'd,"

which so powerfully impels him to search into every thing t
may throw light on his physical and moral existence.

> " 'Tis the Divinity that stirs within us"——

It makes us feel that our soul is immortal ; and it is the agita
produced by this feeling, that makes us very naturally seek
love to dwell on the proofs of our glorious immortal
Hence the delight, which we take in the study of ourselves
of every thing that relates to us, and the efforts, which
make to carry our knowledge as far as the Almighty has
mitted it to extend. He, who created the desire,
knows how to set bounds to our foolish inquiries ; but, lim
as it is, the whole circle, by which our knowledge is bound
is still open to our researches ; and we are yet very far f
having reached its utmost verge.

God has revealed himself to mankind in two ways ; by
sacred writings, and by the works of nature, constantly o
before us ; and it is the privilege as well as the duty of ma
study both to the advancement of his glory. Therefore w
the divine labours to discover the truths, which are conceale
rather veiled under the mysterious language of the former,
philosopher, irresistibly impelled by a similar desire, will
terrogate the latter ; and, with due submission, will view

compare all that can be grasped by his understanding and by his senses. Who knows but that, as this world advances towards its inevitable end, it may have been decreed that the knowledge of man should go on increasing, until the blaze of eternal light should burst at once upon the whole race? But I find I have been involuntarily drawn into the regions of fancy; it is time to turn to the less fascinating topicks which are the subject of these notes.

Yet before I proceed to the Language of the Massachusetts Indians, I may be permitted to shew what fruits have been derived from the pursuit of our science, since it has begun to be considered as an interesting object of study. What great advantage may be derived from it in the end—whether it will enable us to solve the problem of the origin of the population of this continent, facilitate the formation of an universal oral or written language, or lead to some other discovery not yet thought of, though not less important than those that have been mentioned, is yet in the womb of futurity; nevertheless it is certain, that the researches of modern philologists have brought to light many curious and interesting facts, of which our ancestors were entirely ignorant, and by means of which the science has acquired certain fixed points, from whence we may proceed with greater ease to further and more particular investigations.

By the labours of the illustrious Adelung, a census, as it were, has been taken of all the languages and dialects (that are known to us) existing on the surface of the earth. They have been all registered and enumerated, and it is now ascertained, as nearly as possible, that their aggregate numbers amount to 3064; of which Africa has 276, Europe 587, Asia 987, and America (the largest number of all) 1214, being more than Asia and Africa together, and nearly as many as the whole of the old continent, Africa excepted. It is true that in the interior, and, perhaps, even on the coast of the latter country, there are nations yet undiscovered, and whose languages, of course, are not known to us; and in the enumeration of *American* idioms it is easy to perceive, that the same tribes are sometimes registered more than once under different names; but when we consider, that there are also unknown Indian nations on our continent, we shall, by setting off these against those that are variously exhibited, have a tolerable approximation of their numbers and different idioms; and, upon the whole, this inquiry leads us to the almost certain conclusion, that all the languages and dialects of our globe, known and unknown, do not exceed the number of *four thousand*, but, on the contrary, the probability seems to be that they do not reach it.

It is ascertained, at least nothing has yet appeared to the co
trary, that the languages of our American Indians are rich
words and grammatical forms ; that they are adequate to the e
pression even of abstract ideas, and that they have a mode (d
ferent from our own) by which they can easily combine the
radical sounds with each other so as to frame new words, whe
ever they stand in need of them. What is still more extraord
nary, the model of those languages has been found to be th
same from north to south, varieties being only observed in son
of the details, which do not affect the similarity of the gener
system ; while on the Eastern continent languages are foun
which in their grammatical organization have no relation wh;
ever with each other. And yet our American idioms, exce
where they can be traced to a common stock, differ so muc
from each other in point of *etymology*, that no affinity whatev
has been yet discovered between them. The philosopher, wh
considers this wonderful richness of forms in the languages
our Indians, will be apt to think, that it is the first stage of h
man speech ; that all languages have been thus complex
their origin, and have acquired simplicity in the progress of c
vilization ; but if he will only bestow a single look upon th
oral language of the *Chinese*, he will find his system strong
shaken ; for it cannot be civilization, that made this most impe
fect idiom what it is ; and not a single vestige remains in it
shew that it was ever a complex or even a polysyllabick la
guage. On the contrary, it is to be presumed, that if the Chine
were to adopt an alphabetical mode of writing in lieu of the
hieroglyphicks, their oral speech would be found insufficient
least for written communications, and the nation would be co
pelled to adopt new words and new grammatical forms. F
their written characters represent no sounds to the ear, but on
ideas to the mind ; the beauty of their poetry, as well as the
prose, consists in the elegance of the associations of ideas prese
ed to the mind through the *visual* sense ; and their communic
tions through the *ear* serve only for the more common and coai
er purposes of life. What affinity is there then between such
language and those of the Indians of America ; and how can the
be said to be derived from each other ? This is an interesti
problem, the solution of which yet remains to be discovere

It has been, moreover, ascertained that one nation at least
the eastern continent of Asia, the *Sedentary Tschuktschi*, spe;
an *American* language ; a dialect of that, which begins in Gree
land, crosses the American continent, (on both coasts of which
is found among the people called Eskimaux,) is spoken at Noht
Sound, and the mouth of the Anadir, and from thence northwa

along the coast, to the peninsula called *Tschutschkoi Noss*, or the promontory of the *Tschutschki*. On the other hand, no nation has yet been discovered on this continent, that speaks an Asiatick language. The grammatical forms of the languages of the Koriaks, Lamouts, Kamtchadales, and other nations of the eastern coast of Asia, are not yet known to us; and while we are taking pains to investigate the languages of our own country, it is much to be wished, that the learned men of the Russian empire would collect and communicate information respecting those of their Kamtchadale, Samoyed and Siberian tribes; so that a full comparison might be established between them and those of our Indians.

It has been also ascertained, (and the discovery was first partially made by the great navigator Cook,) that from the peninsula of Malacca in Asia to the Cocos Island, a hundred leagues from the coast of Tierra Firme, and through the various clusters of islands in the South Sea, and also in the Island of Madagascar, dialects of the same language (the Malay) are spoken; which, with other indications, has led an ingenious American writer, Dr. McCulloh of Baltimore, to suppose that the South Sea was once a continent, and that America was peopled through that channel.* This question deserves further investigation; and the Malay, as well as its cognate languages, ought to be studied with that view. No traces of this language have been yet discovered on the coast of the American continent; but they may appear on further research.

I should exceed the bounds which I have prescribed to myself, if I were to take notice of all the interesting facts, which the comparative science of languages has brought to light. Nor is this the proper place to do it. My task is that of an annotator of the venerable Eliot's Grammar of the (Massachusetts) Indian language; and my object is to communicate, in aid of this valuable work, some of the most material facts and observations which several careful perusals of its contents, with collateral studies, have disclosed and suggested to me. Among those studies, I have not neglected that of his translation of the sacred writings, from which I have derived a greater insight into the nature, forms and construction of this curious language, than could be obtained from the Grammar alone; for this is by no means so full as it might have been, if the illustrious author, impelled by his zeal for the propagation of the Christian faith, had

* Researches on America, being an attempt to settle some points relative to the Aborigines of America, &c. By James H. McCulloh, junr. M. D. Baltimore, Robinson, 1817. Octavo.

not written it for immediate use, as introductory to the furth
instruction, which he was so well qualified to give to those wl
stood in need of it.   I have had no other view in writing the
notes than to facilitate the labours of my fellow students, a
shall be happy, if my efforts shall prove successful, though but
an inconsiderable degree.

There can be no doubt, that this language is a dialect of th
widely extended idiom which was spoken, with more or lc
variation, by the Souriquois and Micmacs in Nova Scotia, t
Etchemins, who inhabited what is now the State of Maine, t
Massachusetts, Narragansets and other various tribes of the ʎ
mouchiquois* in New England, the Knisteneaux, and Algonki
or Chippeways in Canada, the Mohicans in New York, t
Lenni Lenape, or Delawares, Nanticokes and other nations
the same stock in Pennsylvania and Maryland, and lastly,
the Powhatans in Virginia ; beyond which, to the *southward*, th
race has not been discovered, but extended itself *westward*, t
der various names, such as Kickapoos, Potawatamies, Miamis
Twightwees, &c. to the great river Mississippi ; on the other si
of which the Sioux or Naudowessie, and the language of t
Pawnees, (or Panis,) branching into various dialects, appear
predominate.   On this side, this rich idiom of the Wapanach
or Men of the East, and the Iroquois with its kindred languag
the Huron or Wyandot, and others, enjoyed exclusive swa
while to the southward, towards Louisiana and Florida, a nu
ber of idioms are found, which do not at all appear to be der
ed from each other, such as the Creek or Muskohgee, Chicl
saw and Choctaw, Uchee, (yet unknown, but said to have
character peculiar to itself,) Atacapas, Chatimachas and othe
among which no analogy is to be found by the comparison
their different vocabularies.   The same phenomenon has bc
observed in the kingdom of Mexico ; where several languaɡ
entirely different are crowded together on a small spot, wh
elsewhere, as in Peru, Chili and Paraguay, some one or t
master idioms extend their dominion in various dialects, like c
Wapanachki and Iroquois, to a very great distance.†   Th
remarkable facts will not escape the attention of the philo
pher ; but being foreign to my present subject, I have thouɡ
it sufficient merely to point them out to the observation of the
who feel an interest in these disquisitions.

* The French called the New England Indians by the general name
Almouchiquois or *Armouchiquois*, which name is to be seen in several of
ancient maps.

† The Aztek or Mexican proper, Othomi, Tarascan, Huastecan, &c.

I shall not waste time in proving, by the analogy of words, the strong affinity which exists between the Massachusetts and the Lenape, Algonkin and Mohican languages; of all which the former more or less partakes, not without a mixture of the Souriquois, Etchemin and other Nova Scotia dialects; it is sufficient to quote what my venerable friend, Mr. Heckewelder, wrote to me on the 8th of April, 1819.* "I once had," he says, "Eliot's Bible here for examination, and well understanding the Mohican language, I soon worked myself into the *Natick*, so that I could not only understand the one half of it at least, but became quite familiar with the language. There are certain letters in the words which are changed, as I have already somewhere mentioned to you." This change of letters is noticed by Eliot himself in his Grammar, page 2, where he instances the word *dog*, called *anum* by the Massachusetts proper, *alum* by the Nipmuk, and *arum*, by the northern Indians. The Delawares say *allum*, the Algonkins *alim*, the Etchemins (Indians of Penobscot and St. John's) *allomoos*, and the Miamis *lamah*.† The changes of the consonants *l*, *m*, *n*, and *r* for each other are very frequent in the various dialects of American languages. Thus the Delawares of New Sweden called themselves *Renni Renape*, instead of *Lenni Lenape*, making use of the *r* where the others have the *l*. These variations are very necessary to be attended to in the comparative study of our aboriginal idioms; other instances of them will appear in the course of these notes.

Notwithstanding the strong affinity, which exists between the Massachusetts and these various languages of the Algonkin or Lenape class, is too clear and too easy of proof to be seriously controverted, yet it is certain that a superficial observer might with great plausibility deny it altogether. He would only have to compare the translation of the Lord's prayer into the Massachusetts, as given by Eliot in his Bible, Matthew vi. 9, and Luke xi. 2, with that of Heckewelder into the Delaware from Matthew, in the Histor. Transactions, vol. i. page 439, where he would not find two words in these two languages bearing the least affinity to each other. But this does not arise so much from the difference of the idioms, as from their richness, which afforded to the translators multitudes of words and modes of expressing the same ideas, from which to make a choice; and they happened

---

* The numerous letters and other communications, which I have received from Mr. Heckewelder on the subject of the Indian languages, will be considered at a future day as a most valuable and interesting collection. They are carefully preserved.

† See Barton's New Views, Comparative Vocab. Verbo *Dog*.

not to hit upon the same forms of expression. Thus Eliot tr
lates the words " *Our father which art in heaven,*" by Nꝏshun
sukqut, which literally means, " Our father who art in the st
place, among the great luminaries of the sky," from the D
ware *Gischuch*, the sun, which the Narragansets called *Kees
quand,* and adored it by that name ;* whence Kesuck
Keesuck, (or rather Keesukh with a guttural χ at the end,)
which these nations designated what we call the *sky* or the H
ens, and also the *sun* and *the space of a day.* This NꝏshunKe
qut might easily have been rendered in the Delaware by N
Gischuchink, "*Our father heaven or sun in,*" (the prepositio
being expressed in the Massachusetts by the termination ı
qut, and in the Delaware by *ink*, as is usual in the Indian
guages ;) but Zeisberger and Heckewelder preferred substitu
for the word *Nooch,* which is that by which children add
their natural father, the more elegant word *Wetochemelenk* ;
in turning to Mr. Heckewelder's Correspondence in the Hi
Transactions, p. 421, it will be found, that they had still a ch
of other terms for the same word *father* ; such is the wond
richness of these *barbarous* languages. It may be rema
here, that even Eliot's own translations of the Lord's praye
given in Matthew and Luke, differ from each other more thaı
variations of the text require ; as for instance, in the sente
" Give us this day (or day by day) our daily bread ;" in Matt
this is translated by *Nummeetsuongash asekesukokish* † *assamaiı
yeuyeu kesukod,* which literally means " Our victuals of every
give us *this this* (for energy's sake) day on, or *sun on.*" Aŋ
Luke xi. 2, he translates it thus : *Assamaiinnean kokokesuk
nutasesesukokke*‡ *petukqunneg,* by which the text is literally
dered, in the same order of words : " Give us day by day
daily bread." These observations I have thought it neces
to make, with the expectation that they may be useful to
student, in his comparative views of the Indian languages.
     I ought to observe here also, that the language of Eliot's G
mar may, possibly, not be exactly the same with that of his tr

---

* See Roger Williams' Key, Chap. xii. in 3 Mass. Hist. Col. p. 217.

† *Daily* or every day, every *sun* ; from *kesuk,* sun, as above mentione

‡ I am inclined to believe, that there is here an errour of the press, and
this word should have been printed *nuttasekesukokke,* from *kesuk,* day oı
and the *t* should have been duplicated for the sake of the affixed pronoı
so as to read *nut-ta* or *n'ta,* and not *nu-ta,* &c.

[Mr. *Du Ponceau's* conjecture is well founded. He uses the editi
1680, which, although it is the revised one, is evidently incorrect in th
stance. The edition of 1661 has the word as Mr. Du Ponceau here sup
it should be—*nutasekesukokke.*]

lation of the Bible.   There are some differences in the words, as well as in the forms of speech, which it is indispensable that the student should be aware of.   For instance ; in his Grammar, page 14, he gives the word *nequt*, (from the Delaware *n'gutti*,) to express the numeral *one*, whereas in his Bible he more commonly makes use of *pasuk*, from the Algonkin *pegik* and Chippeway *pashik*.   Thus he says *pasuk cherub*, " one cherub." 2 *Chron*. iii. 11.   *Pasuk ox, lamb, ram*.   *Numb*. xxviii. 27, 28, 29.   " Pasukqunnuoo weyausoo," *one flesh*.   *Gen*. ii. 24.   And so in other places.   As I proceed in my observations upon his Grammar, I shall also shew some differences in the forms.   Yet the two languages (if in fact he did employ more than one dialect) appear to be substantially the same.

This translation of the Bible by our venerable Eliot is a rich and valuable mine of Indian philology.   A complete grammar and dictionary might, with labour and perseverance, be extracted from it ; for there is hardly a mode or figure of speech, which is not to be found somewhere in the sacred writings.   It has been of great use to me in the investigation of the character and structure of the American languages, and I hope to derive still further benefit from it.   Every copy of it, that is yet extant, ought to be preserved with the greatest care, as it is hardly to be hoped that it will ever be entirely reprinted.

It is not, however, every attempt at translation into the Indian languages, that ought to be trusted to by the student.   Indeed, it is but too true, that even simple vocabularies, when not made by persons, who have resided long among the Indians or who are extremely careful and judicious, are in general miserably deficient.   Such is that of the language of the Delawares of New Sweden, published by Campanius Holm at Stockholm in 1696, with Luther's Catechism in Swedish and Indian ; both of which (the vocabulary and the translation) are exceedingly faulty, and betray the grossest ignorance of the language.   Mr. Heckewelder is of opinion, that the writer knew but little of it himself, and that he compiled his work with the aid of Indian traders, by whom he was constantly led into errour.   Some of his mistakes are truly ludicrous.   He translates the words " Gracious God" by *Sweet Manitto ;* but the word *vinckan*, (it should be *wingan*,) by which he attempts to express *sweet*, is one, which, in the Delaware language, is only applied to eatables ; so that the sense, which he conveys to an *Indian*, is that of *O sweet tasted Manitto!* Yet no language is richer in suitable appellations for the Deity.   In the same manner, when he means to express the verb " to love" in a divine sense, he uses the word *tahottamen*, applicable only to the liking, which men have

14

for perishable things, when he had *cholan*, from the substant[i]
ahollowagan, (*love*,) which it is most probable he was un[a]
quainted with. These observations were communicated to [a]
by Mr. Heckewelder, with many others of the same kind ; whi[c]
while they prove the ignorance of the writer of that book,
ford additional evidence of the astonishing richness of o[ur]
Indian languages, and of the multitude of words, by means
which they can discriminate between the most delicate shad[e]
of the same thought. The verb *to love* is still different
but not improperly, expressed by our Eliot : " Womonook ku[m]
matwomoóg," *love one another*. *Matt.* v. 44. This word is de[ri]
ved from *wunnegen, good ;* Delaware *wuliechen,* it is good or w[ell]
done. *Kah kusseh mo ahche wunnegen,* " And behold it was ve[ry]
good." *Gen.* i. 31. From the same root is the word *wunanu[m]*
bless ; *Wunanum Jehovah,* " Bless the Lord." *Ps.* ciii. 1. The[re]
appears to be no end to this rich variety.

I cannot help observing here, that the same richness, not [on]
ly in terms applicable to *physical* subjects, but in *moral* a[nd]
metaphysical terms, is to be found in the southern as well as
the northern languages. Thus in the Huastecan idiom (N[ew]
Spain) we have

> *Canezomtaba,* love, in a general sense.
> *Canezal,* to love (in this sense.)
> *Lehnaxtalah,* love with desire (*amor descando.*)
> *Lehnal,* to love, in this sense (*apetecer.*)
> *Cacnaxtabal,* love with courtship (*amor cortesario.*)
> *Cacnal,* to love, in this sense (*cortejar.*)
> *Cacnax,* a lover, in this sense (*cortejo.*)
>
> ZENTENO'S GRAMMAR, p. 51.

But it is time that I should have done with these gene[ral]
observations. I shall proceed now to remark more directly [on]
the contents of the Grammar, which is the immediate subj[ect]
of these notes.

I. *Alphabet.*

(Gram. p. 1.) *

It is much to be regretted, that the learned have not y[et]
agreed upon some mode of communicating to the ear, throu[gh]
the eye, an uniform impression of the effects of the vario[us]
sounds produced by the human organs of speech. The on[ly]

---

* The reader will observe, that this and the other references to the *Gra[m]
mar* are made to the *original* paging of that work, which is preserved in [the]
margin of the present edition.

way to obtain this desirable end, is for some person endowed with correct judgment and a nice, discriminating ear, to propose an alphabet, or table of signs, which, after a time, cannot fail (with perhaps some slight variations) to be generally adopted. My learned friend, Mr. Pickering, of Salem, in an excellent Essay, lately published in the fourth volume of the *Memoirs of the American Academy of Arts and Sciences,* has broken the ice and proposed an alphabet for our own Indian languages, which has the merit of great simplicity. It is understood, that its principles are to be followed in the publication of several vocabularies, that are to be inserted in the Journal of the late Expedition to the Westward under the command of Major Long, which is shortly to be put to the press by Mr. *Nuttall;* and there is no doubt that his example will be followed by others, particularly by missionaries, to whom the Essay has been transmitted by the missionary societies. If, as there is great reason to expect, Mr. Pickering's orthography gets into general use among us, America will have had the honour of taking the lead in procuring an important auxiliary to philological science.

It is universally admitted, that the alphabets of the principal European nations, which have been hitherto used to represent the sounds of our Indian languages, are inadequate to the purpose. The *English* is anomalous, and its powers not sufficiently determined. Its system of *vowels* is particularly defective. The *French* partakes of the same defects, though in a less degree ; and in other respects is too often apt to mislead, because its consonants are generally unarticulated at the end of words. The *German* is more perfect than either ; but German ears do not sufficiently discriminate between the hard and soft consonants, such as *b* and *p*, *g* hard and *k*, and *d* and *t*, by which considerable confusion is introduced. It will be recollected, that in Zeisberger's Vocabulary of the Delaware, the letter *g* is frequently used as *homophonous* with *k*, because, it is said, the printer had not a sufficient number of types to furnish the latter character as often as it was wanted. Notwithstanding this defect, however, it must be acknowledged that a better idea of the sounds of the Indian languages is given by means of the German alphabet than of any other.

Our author has, of course, made use of the *English* letters to express the sounds of the *Massachusetts* language ; in consequence of which, it is sometimes difficult to recognize even the same words differently spelt by Zeisberger in the *Delaware.* Thus the latter writes *n'dee,* (*my heart,*) which is to be pronounced as if spelt *n'day,* according to the powers of the

English alphabet. Eliot, on the contrary, writes it *nuttah*. Thi makes it appear a different word, in which we scarcely per ceive an analogy with the former. By the first syllable, *nu* he means to express the sounds, which the *German* represent by *n'd*, (perhaps *n't*, for the reason above suggested,) the shor *u* standing for the interval, or sheva, between the two conso nants; which Zeisberger more elegantly represents by an apos trophe. The last syllable, *tah*, is the German *dee* or *tee*, (Englis *day* or *tay*,) the *a* being pronounced acute, as in *grace, face*. our author had selected the diphthong *ay* to express this sound and reserved the *a* to represent its broad pronunciation in *fur car*, the student would have been much better able to perceiv the analogy between the Massachusetts and its cognate idioms But that was not his object; and it was enough for him tha the mode of spelling, which he adopted, was sufficient for hi purpose. Had he taken the other course, *n'dee* and *n'ta* would have been immediately recognized to be the same word while *n'dee* and *nuttah* hardly shew any resemblance. ought to be observed, that, although our venerable grammariar in his alphabet, ascribes the acute pronunciation to the letter *e* (except when it takes its short sound before a consonant,) an generally expresses the broad sound of that letter by *au*, ye there are many words, in which it has the open sound, espe cially when followed by *h:* But this can only be discovere by comparison with other languages, derived from the sam stock.

The *whistled W*, of which he takes no notice, but which it evident exists in the *Massachusetts*, as well as in the other *We panachki* idioms, he represents sometimes by *w* and sometime also by short *u*, as in *uppaumauopoh*, "they did pay him," fo *w'paumauopoh*. This is placed beyond a doubt by the circum stance of the personal pronouns affixed to the verbs; *n'* for th first person, *k'* for the second, and *w'* for the third; being th same in the Delaware and Massachusetts languages. Before *vowel*, he employs the *w*, as in *wantamooh*, "he is not wise and sometimes prefixes the *ꝏ*, as in "*ꝏwadchanumꝏun*," does not keep it. This *ꝏ*, placed before the *w*, was probabl meant to express the peculiarity of the *whistled* sound, by whic he seems to have been not a little embarrassed. I believe once meant to have represented this sound by *vf*, to which ascribes a peculiar pronunciation, different from that of *v save, have*. (See his alphabet, and his observations on the consonant in his Grammar, page 2.) But he does not seem have kept to his purpose; for I do not find the *vf* employe elsewhere, either in his Grammar or in his translation of th

Bible and New Testament, but always either the *w*, the œw or the short *u* when followed by a consonant.

It is remarkable, that our author appropriates no character, or combination of characters, to express the guttural sound of the Greek *χ*, which is very frequent in these languages. This is a defect very common to Englishmen, who attempt to express Indian sounds by the letters of their alphabet. This sound, being entirely wanting in our language, is very often neglected and not at all noticed. In some vocabularies it is expressed by *gh* ; but as these letters are always united in proper English words, it is difficult to know when they are to be pronounced, or are merely used to lengthen the sound of the preceding vowel or diphthong.

The letter *q* is often employed by our author, without any other apparent power than that of *k*, as in " tœhkequn," *heavy*, 1 *Samuel*, iv. 18 ; but he also uses it more properly as in English before *ua* and *uo*, as in *wuskesukquash*, " his eyes," and in *squontamut*, " the gate." *Ibid*. 15, 18.

Upon the whole, this alphabet, though not so perfect as it might be in the eyes of the scholar, appears, nevertheless, to have fully answered the pious purpose of the excellent author ; for he tells us in his Grammar, page 4, that the Indians, by means of it, " soon apprehended and understood this Epitome of the Art of Spelling, and (by its means) COULD SOON LEARN TO READ."

II.   *Noun Substantive.*

(Gram. p. 8.)

OUR author gives but little information on this subject; perhaps there is but little to be given. The genders, as in the Delaware, are not masculine and feminine, but animate and inanimate. Trees, plants, and grasses are in the class of *inanimates ;* which is different from the Delaware, for in that they are classed as *animates*, except annual plants and grasses. 1 *Hist. Trans.* p. 367, 368.

Substantives are not varied by " Cases, Cadencies and Endings," except animates, when governed by a verb transitive, when they end in *oh*, *uh*, or *ah*. The genders are also distinguished by a difference of termination, but merely for the designation of the *plural number*. This termination is *og* in the animate, and *ash* in the inanimate form. In the Delaware, the animate has *ak*, and the inanimate *all* or *wall*. In the Narraganset, the plural

endings are *ock*, *og*, *auock*, for the animate, and *ash*, *anash* fo
the inanimate. *Mithrid.* vol. iii. part iii. page 381.

We are not a little surprised, however, after the positiv
statement of our author, that substantives are not distinguished
by cases, (except as above mentioned,) to find different termi
nations of the same word, in various parts of his translation o
the Bible, of which he makes no mention and gives no expla
nation in his Grammar : *Wuttauoh Zion*, "Daughter of Zion.
Lament. ii. 8.   *Woi Jerusalemme wuttaunin*, "O daughter o
Jerusalem." *Woi penomp Zione wuttaunin*, "O virgin daughte
of Zion." *Ibid.* 13.   *Woi kenaau Jerusaleme wuttaunennk*, "O y
daughters of Jerusalem."   *Solom. Song*, ii. 7.   *Kah ompeta
wuttaneu*, "And she bare a daughter." *Gen.* xxx. 21.

The first of these terminations is correct ; *nuttanoh, kuttanoh
wuttanoh*, "my, thy, his daughter," are the proper nominatives o
this word ; and its being used in the genitive in the passag
cited *(the wall of the daughter of Zion)* does not militat
against the rule laid down ; but the termination *in* in the voca
tive singular, and *unk* in the vocative plural, cannot be accoun
ed for, any more than *eu* in the accusative governed by an ac
tive verb.   The proper plural ending of this word is the an
mate form *og*, which our author frequently employs.   *Qushke
wonk nuttaunog*, "Turn again, my daughters." *Ruth*, i. 1
I am at a loss how to explain these variations, otherwise tha
by the conjecture offered before, that our author might hav
had recourse to different Indian dialects in translating the s
cred writings.   The Delaware has a vocative case, whic
generally ends in *an : Wo Kitanittowian!* O God; *Wo Nihille
lan*, O Lord, &c.   *Zeisberger's MS. Grammar.*

III.   The Article.

It is remarkable, that this language appears to posses
a definite article, although no mention is made of it in th
Grammar. This article is *mo*, contracted from *monko*, an
properly signifies *it.   Kah* MONKO *nnih*, "And IT (was) so.
Gen. i. 7, 9, 11, 24, 30.   *Onk* MO *nnih*, "And IT (was) so.
Ibid. 15.   *Kah kusseh* MO *ahche wunnegen*, "And behold
(was) very good." *Ibid.* 31.

This pronoun, when used as an article, is still further co
tracted into *m*, which, when followed by a consonant, Eli
connects with it by the English short *u*, according to his met
od, and sometimes by short *e*. Thus he writes *metah*, "th
heart," which should be pronounced *m'tah*. It is evident, th

the *m* stands here for an article, because the personal affixes *my, thy, his*, are *n, k*, and *w; nuttah* or *n'tah*, " my heart," *kuttah* or *k'tah*, " thy heart," *wuttah* or *w'tah*, " *his or her heart*," and not *n'mettah, k'mettah, w'mettah*. In the translation of the Bible, this article frequently appears. *Kesteah pakke* METAH, " Create in me a clean heart." *Psalm* li. 10. *Pohqui kah tannogki* METAH, " A broken and contrite heart." *Ibid.* 17. Several words are also found in his Grammar, in which this article is prefixed, though not noticed as such. *Mukquoshim, (m'quoshim,)* a wolf, *muhhog, (m'hog,)* the body, &c. When the personal form is employed, the *m* is left out, and the pronominal affix substituted : *Yeu nuhhog,* " This is my body." *Matt.* xxvi. 36.

This article exists in several of the Indian languages, as in the Othomi, where it is expressed by *na : Na hay,* the earth, *na metzê,* the ice, *na qhi,* the blood, &c.—(See *Molina.*) It appears also in the Algonkin and its cognate idioms : *Mittick, meeteek,* (Algonk. and Chippew.) a tree ; Delaware, *hittuck,* and I think also *m'hittuck* ; Mahican, *metooque* ; Shawanese, *meticqueh* ; all which appear to be the same word.—*Barton's New Views,* verbo *wood.* So also the Mahican, *mooquaumeh,* ice, (Barton ;) Shawanese, *m'quama,* (Johnston ;) Potowatameh, *mucquam,* (Barton ;) Delaware, *m'hockquammi,* (Heckewelder,) and *moseet,* which, in the language of the Indians of Penobscot and St. John's, means *the foot,* (Barton,) and is clearly the Delaware *n'seet, k'seet, w'seet,* (my, thy, his foot,) which Mr. Heckewelder writes *n'sit*, &c., but observes that the *i* is long.*

* Since writing the above notes, I have received an answer to a letter, which I addressed to Mr. Heckewelder on the subject of the *definite article,* a part of speech, which had not been noticed by grammarians in the Indian languages ; and I have now the satisfaction to find, that the opinions above expressed were well founded. The letter also corroborates some of my etymological statements ; and, as it is short, I have thought it best to insert it entire :

" Bethlehem, 23d *August,* 1821.

" MY DEAR FRIEND,

" I HAVE this moment received your favour of the 21st, and having time left sufficient to answer thereto, before the closing of the mail, I comply with your request. The article " *mo*" for *a* or *the*, which you discovered to be prefixed to substantives in the language of the Naticks, is *the same* in the language of the *Lenape*. We frequently leave the letter *m* out, in writing, as the word is well understood without it, and because a reader, not acquainted with the language, might pronounce it too *harsh,* as *em*, or *emdee,* for *the heart.* So it is with other words also, as for instance, in those you quote. The Lenape say, *m'hittuk, the* tree, or *a* tree. The Minsi say, *michtnk, a tree ;* also,

IV. Adjectives.

(Gram. p. 13.)

ADJECTIVES are seldom used singly in the Indian languages, because they are easily compounded with the verb and other parts of speech ; with the *verb* as in the Latin *sapio, frigeo,* &c. and with the *substantive* in a variety of ways, which will be best explained by examples.   I lately sent to Mr. Heckewelder the Empress Catharine's Vocabulary, in the German language, requesting him to fill it up with the same words in the Delaware.   He very kindly complied with my request, but left some blanks in the Indian part, for which he referred me to notes, (also written in German,) which accompanied it.   Among the words thus left blank, were the adjectives OLD and YOUNG, which he said he could not express by terms *sufficiently general.*   The notes on these two words have appeared to me so interesting, and so well calculated to shew the peculiar construction of the Indian languages, that I have thought the reader would not be displeased to have a translation of them.   I shall, therefore, fill up the present article with the valuable information which they contain.

"*Notes on the word* OLD.

"On this I have to observe, that there are many words which it is difficult, and some even impossible to render by terms, which convey precisely the same general idea; the Indians being so very nice in their discriminations, and having words adapted to every shade which they wish to distinguish.   They are particularly attentive to distinguishing between what is animate and what is inanimate.   Sometimes, also, there are words which have a double meaning.   I will give some examples.

m'tachan, wood ;   the Minsi say, *Machtáchan ;* yet both *hittuk* and *táchan* answer the same purpose.

" With regard to the latter part of your letter, I can only repeat what I have in former letters already noticed, viz. that in the Mahicani and other eastern idioms, (the Natick, &c.) the changing of certain letters in words, and the dropping here and there a letter at the end of a word, from that of the mother tongue, (the Lenape,) causes a difference in the writing and speaking, but not in understanding the same, by any person who can speak, or understand the Lenape.   Examples: The Lenape say, *n'dellan,* the Mahicani *n'ténnan,* changing the letter *l* into the letter *n.*   The mail being about to close, I conclude in haste.   I shall write to you further very soon.

JOHN HECKEWELDER."

" The word *old* is employed by us in the most general sense. We say in our languages, *an old man, an old horse, an old dog, an old house, an old basket,* &c. The Indians, on the contrary, vary their expressions, when speaking of a thing that has life and of one that has not; for the latter, instead of the word *old,* they use terms which convey the idea, that the thing *has lasted long,* that it *has been used, worn out,* &c. Of all which take the following examples:

1. *Kíkey,* old, advanced in years (applied to things *animate.*)
2. *Chowíey,* or *chowíyey,* old by use, wearing, &c.

" *Note.* The first syllable in the word *kíkey,* compounded with other syllables, conveys the idea of *parents,* (Lat. *majores;* Germ. *eltern,*) and in brutes is expressive of the stock or race, from which they proceed:

" *Compounds.*

Kíkey, or *kíkeyín,* (*i* long,) to be old, advanced in years.
Kíkeyitschík, old, elderly people.
Kíkeyílenno, an old man, advanced in years.
Kíkeyóchqueu, an old, elderly woman.
Kíkéchum, the old one of the *brute* kind.
Kíkéhelleu, the old ones of the *feathered* tribe.

" There are also *suffixes,* denoting the age of animated beings, which are worthy of remark; as

Mihillúsis, an old man, (Germ. *ein alter Greis;* Fr. *un vieillard, un barbon.*)
Chauchschísis, an old woman, (Germ. *altes mütterchen;* Fr. *vieille bonne femme.*)
Mihillúschum, an old male *quadruped.*
Chauchscháchum, an old female *quadruped.*

" The general words for things *inanimate* are,

Chowíey, or *chowíyey,* (Minsi, *m'chowíey,*) old.
Chowígáwan, an old house, (from *wíkwam,* or *wígwam.*)
Chohagihácan, an old field, (from *hacki,* earth or land.)
Choutæney, an old town, (from *utæney,* or *uteney,* a town.)
Chowáxen, old shoes, (from *maxen,* mockasons, or shoes.)
Chowásquall, old grass, (from *maskik,* grass.)
Chowíey schäkhócqui, old coat, old garment.
15

" There are other words, which denote a thing being old from
use or *wearing ;* as

Metchihilltu, old ; worn out, (as an edged tool.)
Pígihilltu, torn by long use or wearing.
Lógihilltu, fallen to pieces, &c.

" *Notes on the word* YOUNG.

" It is here again difficult to find an adequate general term
as the Indians are always fond of discriminating, and using
words peculiarly applicable to the thing spoken of. As we say
'a new born child or infant,' instead of 'a young child,'
so in Delaware, the word *wuski,* which signifies *new,* is employed to convey the idea of youth ; and they compound it in
the following manner :

Wúski, new, young, (Minsi, *wuskíey.*)
Wúsken, wēsgink, the new.
Wuskilenno, a young man.
Wuskóchquĕu, or *wuskiechquĕu,* a young woman.
Wuskelenápewak, young people.
Wuskchum, a young quadruped.
Wuskigáwan, a new house.
Wuskhagihácan, a new field.
Wuskutœney, a new town.
Wuskhaxen, new shoes.
Wuskíquall, new grass.
Wuskachpoan, new bread, (*achpoan,* bread.)
Wuskítamen, to renew something, &c.

" Although the syllable *wusk,* prefixed to words, serve
both to denote *young* and *new,* yet the Indians have, besides
a variety of other words for distinguishing the young among
animals.   For instance ; their general term for ' the young,'
the immediate offspring, is *nītschān,* (*w'nitschānall,* his or her
young or offspring, who have been brought alive and suckled,
and this applies to man, and beasts of the genus *Mammalia;*
but when they speak of the *feathered* kind, or when the
young is produced from the egg by hatching, they say, *anīn-
schihillĕu ;* plural, *aninschihilleisak ;* barely implying that the
animals are *young feathered creatures.*   See *Zeisberger's De-
aware Spelling Book,* p. 100."

V. Pronouns.

(Gram. p. 7.)

THE personal pronouns in the Massachusetts, as in the Delaware language, are divided into separable and inseparable; and their etymology may be clearly traced to the same source. They are in the two languages as follows:

MASSACHUSETTS.		DELAWARE.
I,	*Neen.*	*Ni.*
Thou,	*Ken.*	*Ki.*
He *or* she,	*Noh* or *nagum.*	*Nacama*, or *neka.*
We,	*Neenawun*, or *kenawun.*	*Niluna*, or *kiluna.*
Ye,	*Kenaau.*	*Kiluwa.*
They,	*Nahoh*, or *nagoh.*	*Necamawa.*

The *inseparable* pronouns, personal and possessive, are the same in both languages; *n* representing the first person, *k* the second, and *w, o,* or *oo,* (as euphony may require,) the third, both in the singular and plural numbers.

The *particular plural* of the *Delawares,* or the *American* plural, as Mr. *Pickering* very properly calls it, has excited much attention among philologists. Our author makes no mention of this distinction; yet there is great reason to believe, that it exists in the *Massachusetts* idiom. In the Delaware, the particular plural, though not mentioned in Mr. *Zeisberger's* Grammar, is expressed by *niluna*, which means *we, some of us,* with relation to a particular number of persons. It is to be observed, that it begins with the letter *n*, indicative of the *first* person; which, being repeated in the last syllable *na*, seems as if it meant to say, *we, we;* that is, *we,* particularly speaking, but not all; whereas the *general* plural, *kiluna,* (*we, all of us,*) begins with the pronominal affix of the *second* person, as if to say, *we and you,* or *we you and all.* The same difference is found in the *Massachusetts,* where *we* is expressed in two modes, *neenawun* and *kenawun;* the one in the same manner beginning with the affix of the *first* person, afterwards repeated, and the other with that of the *second* person; from whence, and the great affinity of the two languages, I strongly conjecture, that NEENAWUN means the particular, and KENAWUN the general plural. This might, I dare say, be ascertained by searching for examples in our author's translation of the Bible; but these notes having been called for sooner than I expected, I have not time at present for the investigation. If the rules of analogy are not deceptive, it will be found, I believe, that I am right in my conjecture.

Our author does not speak of a *dual* number; nor is it probable there is any, other than the *particular plural*.

The question whether all the Indian languages have the *particular plural*, or some of them the *dual* in lieu of it, is an interesting one. I at first inclined to the former opinion; but recent inquiries make the latter seem the most probable. In one of them, at least, (the *Cherokee*,) it appears that there is a *dual* number. Mr. *Pickering*, in consequence of the general remarks on this subject, in the *Transactions of the Historical and Literary Committee*, was led to conjecture, that what had been called the *dual* in the Cherokee, was in fact only the *particular* or *limited plural*, which is common to other Indian dialects. But he has since informed me, that upon conversing on this point with an intelligent young man of that nation, (who is perfectly familiar with our own language,) he has ascertained that this opinion was unfounded, and that the Cherokee language has a proper *dual number*, like the languages of antiquity. There are varieties in the polysynthetick forms of the Indian languages, which do not, however, affect their general character. Absolute uniformity is not to be found in any of the works of nature; and there is no reason why languages should be excepted from this universal rule.

The interrogative pronoun, as our author denominates it, *howan*, plural *howanig*, (*who*,) is also found in the Lenni Lenape. Zeisberger and Heckewelder spell it *auwen*, which, according to the German pronunciation, gives the same sound, except the *h* at the beginning. This pronoun, in the Delaware, is formed into a verb in the following curious manner, which I extract from Zeisberger's MS. Grammar:

From Auwen, who

Singular. *Ewenikia*, who I am.
Ewenikian, who thou art.
Ewenikit, who he is.

Plural. *Ewenikiyenk*, who we are.
Ewenikiyek, who you are.
Ewenikichtit, who they are.

It is worthy of remark, that this nation, whose language (as I shall hereafter have occasion to observe) wants the substantive verb, *I am*, has come so near it, as in these examples, without being able to find it. It is said that they cannot translate into it the sublime sentence in Exodus iii. 14, I AM THAT I AM. This pronominal verb would, it seems, admirably express the last member of it, at least in the sense of the Vulgate translation, *Ego sum qui sum.* These are anomalies, which further study and inquiry may, perhaps, enable us to reconcile.

The demonstrative pronoun *yeu* is in Delaware *yun;* and, upon the whole, there is a great resemblance, in this part of speech, between the two languages. But neither *Eliot* nor *Zeisberger* have expatiated sufficiently upon it. Indeed, these languages are so rich in forms, that a complete grammar of any of them would be too voluminous for common use.

VI. *Verbs.*

(Gram. p. 15.)

THE Verb is the triumph of human language. Its fundamental idea is that of existence; *I am, sum.* This abstract sentiment receives shape and body from its combination with the various modifications of being, by action, passion and situation, or manner of existing; *I am loving, loved, sleeping, awake, sorry, sick;* which the Latin tongue more synthetically expresses by *amo, amor, dormio, vigilo, contristor, ægroto.* Next come the accessary circumstances of person, number, time, and the relations of its periods to each other; *I am, thou art, we are, I was, I shall be, I had been, I shall have been.* Here the Latin again combines these various ideas in one word with the former ones; *sum, es, sumus, eram, ero, fueram, fuero.* Sometimes it goes further, and combines the negative idea in the same locution, as in *nolo;* this, however, happens but rarely; and here seem to end the verbal powers of this idiom. Not so with those of the *Indian* nations. While the Latin combines but few adjectives under its verbal forms, the Indians subject this whole class of words to the same process, and every possible mode of existence becomes the subject of a verb. The *gender* or *genus,* (not, as with us, a mere division of the human species by their sex, but of the whole creation by the obvious distinction of animate and inanimate,) enters also into the composition of this part of speech; and the object of the active or transitive verb is combined with it by means of those *forms,* which the Spanish-Mexican grammarians have called *transitions,* by which one single word designates the person who acts, and that which is acted upon. The *substantive* is incorporated with the verb in a similar manner : thus in the Delaware, *n'matschi*, "I am going to the *house*, I am going *home ;*" *nihillapewi*, "I am my own *master*, I am free ;" *tpisqui-hilleu*, "the *time* approaches," (*properat hora*.) The *adverb* likewise : *nachpiki*, "I am so *naturally ;*" *nipahwi*, "to travel *by night*," (*noctanter ;*) *pachsenummen*, "to divide (something) *equally*," &c. In short, every part of speech in these languages is capable of being associated with the verb and compounded with it, by means of its various inflexions and forms. What shall we say of the reflected, compulsive, meditative, communicative, reverential, frequentative and other circumstantial verbs, which are found in the idioms of New Spain, and other American Indian languages? The mind is lost in the contemplation of the multitude of ideas thus expressed at once by means of a single word, varied through moods, tenses, persons, affirmation, negation, transitions, &c. by regular forms and cadences, in which the strictest analogy is preserved! Philosophers may, if they please, find here proofs of what they have thought proper to call *barbarism ;* for my part, I am free to say, that I cannot so easily despise what I feel myself irresistibly compelled to admire.

It is to be regretted, that our venerable author has given but few Paradigms of the conjugations of the verbs in the Massachusetts language. There are, in fact, in this Grammar, but three—the active verbs *to keep* and *to pay*, and the neuter verb *to be wise ;* the two first of which are conjugated through their negative and transitive forms, and the latter only in the affirmative and negative. He makes us acquainted with the interrogative mood, and prescribes the form of conjugating verbs through it; but, beyond that, the information which he gives, on the subject of this part of speech, is very scanty; while Zeisberger, on the contrary, in his MS. Grammar, has given us a profusion of the *Delaware* verbs, regularly conjugated, which will be found to afford much assistance to the student, and give him a great insight into the manner of compounding and conjugating verbs in these languages.

Whether there are any, or how many, different forms of conjugation in this language, does not appear. In the *Delaware* there are eight, distinguished by the terminations of their infinitive, or of the first person of the present tense of the indicative mood. Zeisberger enumerates them as follows:

The 1st ending in *in* ;	n'dappin, *to be there.*
The 2d in *a* ;	n'da, *I am going.*
The 3d in *elendam* indicates a disposition of the mind ; . . . . }	niwelendam, *I am sad.*
The 4th in *men* ;	gattamen, *I request.*
The 5th in *an* ;	ahoalan, *to love.*
The 6th in *e* or *we* ;	n'dellowe, *I say.*
The 7th in *in*, but used only in the transitive forms ; . . . . }	miltin, *to give.*
The 8th in *on* ;	n'peton, *I bring.*

The moods and tenses of these two languages appear to be the same, though differently classed by their grammarians. Eliot divides the subjunctive mood into two, the optative and suppositive, each having but one tense, which Zeisberger calls the present and conditional tenses of the conjunctive. Our author takes no notice of the *participles*, which the other includes under the infinitive mood. They are numerous, and susceptible of various transitions and forms. Thus the verb *gauwin*, " to sleep," besides having three tenses in the infinitive, to wit, the present, *gauwin*, the past or preterite, *gauwineep*, " to have slept," and the future, *gauwintschi*, which cannot be rendered into English, but in Latin *dormiturus esse*, has the following participles : present, *gewit*, "sleeping ;" (plural, *gewitschik*) preterite, *gewitup*, " having slept ;" plural, *gewitpannik*. The future is given in other verbs. Examples of the conjugation of the participle of the causative verb, through the transitive forms, are given in the *Historical Transactions*, vol. i. p. 416, which I think unnecessary to repeat here. I have no doubt, that these forms substantially exist in the Massachusetts idioms ; but our author's Grammar is by far too much abridged to admit of their being exhibited.

The formation of the *future* tense of the indicative mood is different in the Massachusetts and Delaware languages. In the former, it is expressed by the auxiliaries *mos* and *pish* ; as, *kah pish kuttâyim*, " and thou shalt make ;" *kah pish neemunumwog gold*, " and they shall take gold ;" *kah pish kupponamunash*, " and thou shalt put." *Exod.* xxviii. 2, 5, 12. In the Delaware, the future is designated by the termination *tsch* ; as in *n'pomsi*, " I go ;" future, *n'pomsitsch*, " I shall or will go." In the negative form, this termination is sometimes attached to the conjunction *not* ; as *mattatsch n'dawi*, " I shall not go," for *matta n'dawitsch*. This is one of the elegancies of the language ; very different, however, from any thing that we have seen or heard of in the idioms of the old world.

We must not expect, in these languages, to find any thing like the Greek aorists, or those nice distinctions of time and its different periods in relation to each other, which are found in the learned tongues. The varieties of the Indian verbs are applied to other objects. I do not mean to speak, however, of the *Mexican* languages, in which the verbs are conjugated through all the forms, moods and tenses of the Latin. There you find the imperfect, preterite, pluperfect and even the gerunds in *di, do, d.*, and the supine.[*] I have observed elsewhere, that those who write Indian grammars strive too much to assimilate the forms of those languages to their own or to the Latin, whereas they have a grammar peculiar to themselves, which ought to be studied and explained. The curious and not very natural coincidence, which the Spanish grammarians have almost generally found between the Latin forms and those of the languages of their Indians, inclines me to suspect the accuracy of those writers. It is, nevertheless, evident, that the *southern* idioms have more tenses in their verbs, or forms of conjugation in relation to time, than those of the more *northern* tribes ; in which latter I have only, as yet, been able to discover the present, past and future.

I observed, in my Report to the Historical Committee on the subject of the Indian languages, (*Hist. Trans.* p. xl.) that it appeared to me, that they were generally destitute of the auxiliary verbs *to be* and *to have ;* which I shewed to be the case not only in our own northern, but in the Mexican and Othomi idioms. I added, on the authority of Father Zenteno, that the Mexicans could not translate into their language the sublime sentence, " I AM THAT I AM." *Exod.* iii. 14. In this sentiment I am confirmed, at least as far as concerns the *Wapanachki* languages, by our venerable author, who expressly says, in page 15 of his Grammar, "We" (the Massachusetts) " have no *compleat distinct word* for the *Verb Substantive*, as other, *learned Languages*, and our *English Tongue* have ; but it is under a *regular composition*, whereby *many words* are made *Verb Substantive*."

This curious fact early attracted the notice of the Honourable Judge Davis, of Boston, who, in a letter to me of the 26th o

---

[*] In Basalenque's Tarascan Grammar, pages 33 and 34, under the verb *pani*, " to carry," (*ilevar*,) are the following paradigms:

Gerund in *di*, Pàquaro ésti—*tiempo de llevar.*
———— in *do*, Pàparin—*llevando.*
———— in *dum*, Pàni-niràhara—*roy à llevar.*
Supine in *um*, Hichen himbô éscu pàni—*à me me combiene llevar.*
———— in *u*, Pàquanhàxeti—*cosa digna de ser llevada.*

March, 1819, suggested some doubts upon the subject; and this circumstance led to a correspondence with the Rev. Mr. Heckewelder and the Rev. Mr. Denckе, which I think sufficiently interesting to warrant the insertion of some extracts from their communications in this place.

I shall extract, in the first place, from Judge Davis's letter, who wrote as follows:

" At present I will only suggest a difficulty, which occurs in relation to a remark in page xl. of your *Report* concerning the substantive verb *to be*, in the American languages. I have a manuscript Vocabulary of the language of the Southern or Old Colony Indians of Massachusetts, (compiled by *Josiah Cotton, Esq.* missionary to those Indians early in the last century,) in which the verbs *to be* and *to have* are expressed in a variety of modifications. I have only room for the infinitive moods of these verbs, and the indicative mood, present tense, with numbers and persons:

' Ainneat, to be.

' *Nermont*, I am.	*Nenauunyeu*, we are.*
Kennont, thou art.	*Kenauna*, you are.
Nohne, he is.	*Nâgna*, they are.

' Ahtounnat, to have.

' *Nummahche*, I have.	*Nenauun nummahche*, we have.
Kummahche, thou hast.	*Kenau kummahche*, you have.
Noh mahche, he has.	*Nag mahche*, they have.'

" In Eliot's Bible, the sublime passage (Exod. iii. 14.) *I am that I am*, is thus translated: *Nen nuttinniin nen nuttinniin.* Galatians iv. 12, *I am as ye are*, is thus rendered: *Nen neyane kenaau.* How is the first of these expressions to be grammatically resolved, if there be no *substantive verb* in the language? The last quotation is elliptical in the Greek κἀγὼ ὡς ὑμεῖς; and so it is in the Indian, which, literally, would be, *I as you. Nen* I take to be a pronoun, and so is *kenaau*............I find, in A. Fabre's Grammar of the Chili Language, the following sentence : ' *Los nombres abstractos, como* bondad, blancura, &c. *se hacen posponiendo el verbo* sum, es, est, *à los adjetivos ò sub-*

---

* The original MS. of Cotton has here *Kenauun yeu ;* which, agreeably to Mr. Du Ponceau's opinion, (in his remarks on the Pronouns,) was the *general* plural ; *nenaun yeu* being the *particular* or *limited plural.*—EDITOR.

stantivos.'—Molina, I believe, has a similar remark; but the doctrine is not so distinctly announced as by *Fabres*, to whom *Molina* appears to have been principally indebted for his observations on the language of *Chili*.—*Jean de Laet* also gives us the substantive verb in the *Brazilian* language; aico, *je suis* eroico, *tu es*, oico, *il est* oroico, *nous sommes*, peico, *vous estes* auraè oico, *ils sont*.   In the third person plural, only, the pronoun is prefixed; whereas, in the example from Cotton's MS (whose Vocabulary, I find, has generally a close correspondence with the *Natick*,) we notice the pronouns throughout.   On this subject of the *substantive verb*, and especially of its application in the admirable language of *Chili*, I had some floating ideas, which I had digested into a sort of theory.   Schemes of thought are not always readily abandoned; but I find mine not a little disturbed by the remark in that part of your discussion.   I may hereafter communicate to you the views to which I refer."   Judge Davis adds, in a Postscript to his letter, the following remark: " Eliot often expresses *I am* by the word *nen* alone; but is it not because the phrase is often elliptical in the Greek? In John viii. 58, ' Before Abraham was I AM' is thus rendered: *Negonne onk Abrahamwi nutāpip*.   The expression there is not elliptical in the original; the word *nutāpip* consider as corresponding to ἐγω εἰμί, though I am not able to trace its origin."

This doubt, suggested from so respectable a quarter, and supported, besides, with so much learning and ingenuity, made me distrust my own opinion, and led me to inquire further into the matter.   Still I could not help believing, as I am yet inclined to think, that the want of the substantive verb was a general rule in the Indian languages.   I knew too well the inclination of grammarians to assimilate those idioms to their own, to be shaken by paradigms, in which the verb *sto*, for instance, might be translated by *sum* or *I am*, for want of sufficient attention to the shade of difference between them; but the words *Nen nuttiniin nen nuttiniin*, by which our author had rendered *I am that I am* in his translation of the Bible, though they might not have the precise meaning of the original text, must yet mean something; and I was curious to know by what analogous mode of expression the venerable apostle had got out of this immense difficulty, when he himself had told his readers, that there was " *no compleat distinct word for the Verb Substantive*" in the language.*   I therefore determined to con-

* Grammar, p. 15.

sult my oracle, Mr. Heckewelder, from whom I speedily received an answer, of which I shall here communicate some extracts :

"8th April, 1819.

" I cannot believe, that any of the tribes connected with the *Lenni Lenape* can translate into their language the words *I am that I am,* so as to come up to the same meaning. The late David Zeisberger and myself sought many years in vain for this substantive verb. We had the best chapel interpreters, I may say orators, some of whom were not at a loss to interpret critically almost all scripture passages and expressions ; yet with regard to the one in question, they never came up to the meaning, but made use of the best substitute they could ; for instance : *I abtschi gutteli n'dellsin,* ' I always act the same ;' *elsia, natsch abtschi n'dellsin,* 'so as I do, I shall always do,' or ' I shall always act the same ;' or again, *elinaxia abtschitsch n'dellinaxin,* ' as I appear, (*am* to appearance,) I shall always be.' I cannot find a single instance in the language, in which the verb *I am* is used by itself, that is to say, uncombined with the idea of the act about to be done."

" You have, no doubt, observed, in my *Historical Account,* page 232, that the Indian, striking his breast, says with conscious pride, I AM A MAN. This he expresses by the words *Lenno n'hackey;* literally, *my body is a man* (or, ' I am a man body,' in the sense that we say, *She is a clever body, a young, a handsome body.*) I might then translate ' I am that I am' by *n'hackey iabtschi n'hackey,* ' my body (is) always my body.'—This word *n'hackey,* with the Indians, is a most expressive word. In the Indian song, of which I have given a translation, (*Hist. Trans.* p. 204,) the sentence at the beginning, *O poor me!* is expressed in Indian by *Wo gettemaki n'hackey !* 'O poor my body !' &c.

" All I can say, at present, of Eliot's translation of ' I am that I am' by *Nen nuttinniin nen nuttiniin* is, that it can never be a literal translation of the text. The passage in Galatians iv. 12, ' I am as ye are,' which Eliot translates by *Nen neyane kenaau,* I presume means, ' *I look like you, we are alike, or we look like one another.* I suppose a Delaware translator would say, *Elinaxi-yek, nepe n'delinaxin ;* that is, ' as ye are, so I am also ;' but this is always said in the sense of personal appearance, shape, face, countenance, size, &c. He might have said, also, *n'gutti ktellinaxihhena,* ' we look alike,' ' we look one,' or, *n'gutteli k'delsihhena,* ' we do, act, alike ;' or, lastly, *ni n'dellsin elsiyek,* ' I do as ye do,' &c."

In the same letter Mr. Heckewelder enclosed to me a copy of one he had received from the Rev. Mr. *Dencke*, of Lititz, to whom he had written on the same subject. I trust I shall be excused for translating here some extracts from this letter also, which is written in German:

" I have never known," says Mr. Dencke, " the verb *to be* to exist, either in the Delaware or Chippeway language, and I can find nothing in those idioms that expresses it literally. The nearest to it is (in the Delaware) *ni n'dellsin elsia,* ' as I do.' The pronoun *ni* is duplicated to strengthen the expression of the idea of the first person of the verb ; *elsia* is contracted from *elgiqui,* ' as,' and *lissia,* ' as I do,' (*da ich thue.*) Out of this pronoun *ni,* or *nen,* perhaps, a new verb might be framed, which, I am inclined to think, Mr. Eliot has done in the Natick. This was easy to be done ; but such a word *is not genuine Indian.* I have been, in vain, trying to understand the meaning of *Nen nuttinniin nen nuttinniin,* which appears to be the same sentence twice repeated, but have not been able to succeed————."

" *Ni n'delinaxin elinaxia,* ' as I appear so I am,' (*Ich bin dem so gleich, so wie ich bin.*) But this is not answering Mr. Du Ponceau's question. I should probably express ' I am as ye are,' by *Ni n'dellsin elsiyeek ;* and I do not think that there is any thing that comes nearer to it.

" I think we must remain where we are ; agreeing, however, upon this point, that in the Indian languages that we are acquainted with, ' *I am that I am'* cannot be literally expressed, but a substitute must be employed," &c.

In a Postscript, which follows the copy of Mr. Dencke's letter, Mr. Heckewelder concludes, that if *Nen nuttinniin nen nuttinniin* means any thing, it must be either " I am a man, I am a man," or, " I do so, I do so."

After much consideration and study of the subject, I incline much to the opinion, that Mr. Heckewelder is right in his last conjecture ; and, as it appears to be full time to put an end to these Notes, and the remaining parts of speech suggest no interesting observations, I shall conclude with stating the grounds upon which this conjecture is founded.

It appears to me, in the first place, that the Massachusetts verb *nuttinniin* is the same with the Delaware verb *n'dellsin,* ' I do or act,' which the Germans not unfrequently spell *n'tellsin,* confounding the *t* with the *d,* because their ears do not sufficiently distinguish between the two sounds. Now the first syllable of *nuttinniin*, 'nut,' in which the short *u* is employed to express the interval or *sheva* between the two consonants, is the same with the Delaware *n'd* or *n't ;* the middle syllable *tin* is the Delaware *tel* or *del*, changing *e* into *i* and *l* into *n ; in* is the termination of the verbal form in the Massachusetts, which in this word is the same as in the Delaware ; and *nen* is the duplication of the personal pronoun, for the sake of greater energy, as Mr. Dencke has very properly observed.

This etymological deduction would not prove much, without shewing that the verb *nuttinniin* means " to do or act" in the Massachusetts, as *n'dellsin* does in the Delaware. This, I think, can be done by recurring to examples in our author's translation of the Bible. For instance : *To kittinheh,* "What is it that thou hast done unto me?" *Gen.* xii. 8. *To* means " what ;" *kittinheh* is probably the interrogative form of the verb *nuttinniin,* or *n'tinniin, k't, kut,* or *kit,* being the affix form of the second person, which the letter *k* represents in the Massachusetts as well as in the Delaware. *To kutussem ?* "What hast thou done ?" *Gen.* iv. 10. Here the verb is employed in another form, not being combined with the idea of *to me,* which appears expressed in the former word by the *n,* descriptive of the first person. This is, however, but my humble conjecture, which I offer with great diffidence, after the question has been given up by those who are much more skilled than I am in the Indian languages ; of which I profess to know nothing except the little I have acquired in the solitude of the closet.

I have only to add a remark respecting the verb *nutāpip,* which, as Judge Davis observes, (in the Postscript to his letter,) is used for *I am,* in Eliot's Bible : " *Before Abraham was, I* AM—*Negonne onk Abrahamwi nutāpip.* John viii. 58." At the time when Judge Davis wrote to me, I could not explain the meaning of *nutāpip ;* but I am now able to do it. *N'dappin* is a Delaware verb, which signifies *to be* (in a particular *place*) *stare ;* the preterite is *n'dappineep*, stabam, hic stabam. There can be no doubt but Eliot's *nutāpip,* that is to say, *n'tāpip* or *n'dāpip,* is a contraction of the Delaware *n'dappineep,* and means, *I was there.*

———

SUPPLEMENTARY OBSERVATIONS.   BY THE EDITOR.

AFTER the *Notes and Observations* of Mr. Du Ponceau had been delivered to the printer, I employed the few leisure moments, which I could command, in considering some of the points discussed in them; and in the course of my inquiries some unexpected facts came under my notice. These suggested reflections, which led to a further correspondence between Mr. Du Ponceau and Mr. Heckewelder; and as this correspondence throws much light upon the structure of the Indian Languages, I have thought it would be useful to state in this place some of the facts, to which I have alluded, together with the substance of their additional remarks upon them.

I. On the Verb To BE.

IT will be recollected, that in conformity with what has been observed in modern times, by Dr. *Edwards* in the *Mohegan* language and by Mr. *Zeisberger* and Mr. *Heckewelder* in the *Delaware*, the author of the present Grammar had said a century and a half ago of the *Massachusetts* language—"We have no *compleat distinct word* for the Verb Substantive, as other, learned languages, and our English tongue have; but it is under a regular composition, whereby many words are made verb substantive;" which kind of "composition," he adds, takes place in *nouns, adnouns, adverbs,* or the like.

Notwithstanding this emphatick observation, however, the venerable author, in his version of the Scriptures, had repeatedly found occasion to translate the verb *to be*, and accordingly often attempted to render it by some equivalent Indian word; a striking instance of which is to be found in the passage already brought under discussion in the preceding *Notes : I am that I am,* " Nen nuttinniin nen [*or* ne] nuttinniin."[*] This circumstance led me to examine some of the passages, in which the verb *to be* occurred in the English version of the

---

[*] Eliot's *first* edition has *nen nuttinniin* NE *nuttinniin ;* but the *second* has *nen* in both places. This difference will not affect the reasoning respecting the substantive verb, but will only make a difference in the grammatical analysis of the sentence.

Bible; and I soon found, that Eliot appeared to have been driven to the necessity of resorting to Indian words, apparently very different from each other.   For one example of this we need not go beyond the very text above cited; where, though in the first part of the verse he employs the expression *Nen* NUTTINIIN for *I am*, yet, in the latter part, he uses the words *Nen* UKOH :   I AM *hath sent me unto you*—"*Nen ukoh* anœteamwe nuttanœnuk en kuhhogkáœnt."   In other parts of his version he uses various other forms of expression for the different tenses of the English verb; as will be seen in the following examples :

Gen. iii. 9. Where art thou ?	Toh *kutapin ?*
—— v. 24. And he was not.	Kah mattah na *wutápéin.*
—— xviii. 24. For the fifty righteous that are therein.	Newutche napannatahshinchagodtog sampwesecheg na *apitcheg.*
Exod. viii. 21. And also the ground whereon they are.	Kah wame ohkeit ne *aphettit.*
—— xx. 21. Where God was.	Ne God *apit.*
1 Sam. xix. 3. Where thou art.	Uttoh *apean.*
1 Kings xxii. 4. I am as thou art.	Nen *netatuppe* ken.
Job xxxviii. 4. Where wast thou ?	Uttoh *kutaphneas ?*
Psalm xxxvii. 36. And lo he was not.	Kah kusseh matta *ohtano.*
Isa. xxiii. 13. This people was not, till the Assyrian, &c.	Yeug missinninnuog *matta appupuneg* noh pajeh Assyriansog, &c.
John viii. 58. Before Abraham was I am.	Negonne Abrahamwi, *nutapip.*
Rev. i. 4, 8, & iv. 8. From him which is, and which was and which is to come.	Wutch noh noh *koh,* noh *koh* mô, noh *paont.*
—— xvii. 8. The beast that was and is not and yet is.	Puppinashimwoh, noh mo, kah noh matta, kah noh yeuyeu *apit.*

In many other places, however, the author uses some form of the word *nuttiniin :*

Gen. xxxi. 40. Thus I was ; in the day the drought consumed me and the frost by night.	Yeu *mo nuttinaiin*, kesukodae kusittau nuttônauûshik, ka tohpu nukonáeu.
—— xxxi. 41. Thus I have been twenty years in thy house.	Yeu *nuttinaiin* neesneehage ko tumwae kekit.

This apparent diversity in the modes of expressing the same idea excited my curiosity. It was manifest that the venerable author had experienced a difficulty in finding what he calls in his Grammar, a "*complete*" verb substantive; and that he had been obliged to content himself with words which only approximated to the strict signification of that verb. I therefore endeavoured to ascertain the precise import of the words, which he thus appeared to have used as substitutes for it. With this view, I began to read *Cotton's English and Indian Vocabulary*, (the MS. mentioned in the *Introductory Observations* to the present Grammar,) from which the Hon. Judge Davis had extracted the example of the verb *to be*, that had given rise to the discussion in Mr. Du Ponceau's Notes.* In the course of my reading, I soon met with the verb *nuttiniin*, used by Eliot, in Exod. iii. 14. But was not a little surprised at the same time to find, that Cotton translated it, not by our verb *to be*, but by the verb *to become*. He gives it in this form :

" I am become, ... nuttinni.
We are become, ... —— yumun.
To become, ... unniinat."

This discovery now led me to examine Eliot's Bible for texts where the verb *to become* occurred; in order to see how far *Eliot* agreed with *Cotton*, in rendering that English verb; and I found, that he also had rendered it sometimes by *nuttinniin*, the very word, which he had in other places used for the verb *to be*.

Upon returning to my examination of *Cotton's Vocabulary*, I soon met with another of Eliot's substitutes for the verb *to be*—the word *nutapip*, which occurs in this text : *Before Abraham was I am*—" Negonne onk Abrahamwi *nutapip*," John viii. 58. But here again I found that *Cotton* had affixed

* See page xxxv. of the Notes.

to the Indian word a different idea from that which *Eliot*
seemed to have done ; for *Cotton* explained *nutapip* by our
verb *to be able*, in different modes and tenses as follows :

" I am able, ... nuttâppĭnum.
Thou art able, ... ken kuttâppĭnum.
He is able, ... nagum tâppĭnnum.
We are able, ... nuttâppinnumūmun.
Ye are able, ... kuttâppinnumumwœ.
They are able, ... nâg tappinumwog, &c.
I was able, ... nuttâppinūmup.
Thou wast able, ... kuttâppinūmup.
Be thou able, ... ken tapinish.
Let him be able, ... noh tapinetch.
Let us be able, ... tapinumuttuh.
Be ye able, ... tapinnumōŏk.
Let them be able, ... tapinnumhittitch.
Art thou able? . . . . sun kuttapinnum ?
To be able, ... tapinumunat."

As I had discovered these various explanations of the Indian words in question, in the same manuscript where the
Hon. Judge Davis had found the supposed substantive verb
(*ainneat*) which had given occasion to the discussion in
the preceding Notes, I communicated to Mr. Du Ponceau the
facts, which had thus fallen under my observation, and referred him to several texts of Eliot's Bible, where the words in
question occurred ; requesting him, at the same time, to favour me with his reflections on the subject ; for whether
Cotton was right in translating *nuttinniin* by *become*, while
Eliot had rendered it by our verb *to be*, was a point which
my own acquaintance with the language did not enable me
to determine.

Mr. Du Ponceau, in his reply to my letter, (after observing,
that " perhaps *Cotton* could find no better word for *become*")
says—" But if the word means strictly and precisely *become*,
how can it mean TO BE in the text, *I am that I am?* Eliot's
translation would then be—*I become, I become.* This is still
farther from the meaning of his text than the Delaware
n'dellsin, I AM so.*　If I may indulge a conjecture, I should

* See Mr. Du Ponceau's Notes, p. xxviii.

17

say, that the *Wapanachki* had no proper word for either *be* or *become*, and have perhaps used the same *approximation* in both cases.   In general, it appears to me, that the idea of *existence* is never presented singly in any Indian word, but always coupled with some accessary idea, which connects the word with what is to follow.   Thus, if they meant to say *I have now become good*, they would probably say, *I am now so that I am good*, or use a word implying or leading to that compound idea.   It is true, the relation *back* to what I formerly was, does not here appear; and there lies the difficulty."   Mr. Du Ponceau, however, without expressing a settled opinion of his own, consulted Mr. Heckewelder, and has obligingly furnished me with their correspondence; the substance of which I cannot communicate to the reader in a more useful and interesting form than their own language.

In the first letter which Mr. Du Ponceau wrote to Mr. Heckewelder (Oct. 8, 1821) he made the following inquiries : "I wish to know how you express the word *become* in Delaware, as thus : *I was once bad, I have now become good* ; and these Scriptural phrases :

The man is become *as one of us.*   Gen. iii. 22.
What will become *of his dreams ?*   Gen. xxxvii. 20.
What is become *of him ?*   Exod. xxxii. 1.
To them gave he power to become *the sons of God.*   John i. 12.

"In the Natick, (or Massachusetts,) Eliot expresses this word by *nuttinniin*, the same which he uses for *I am that I am*. I think this word is derived from the Delaware *n'dellsin, n'tellsin*, changing the *l* into *n*, which is very frequent among Indians.   If the Delawares use *n'dellsin* for *become*, it will confirm me in my opinion.

"In the short History of the Bible, at the end of Zeisberger's Spelling Book, it seems to me I have found the word *become* expressed by *n'dellsin*.   See page 127, line 10—*That they would* become *too powerful*.   It seems to me that the word *wtellitsch*, in the translation, is meant to express *become*. See also page 136, line 9—*wtellitsch sokenapalan*.   Does not this mean, *should be*, or *become* baptized?   You will find the word *become* in several other parts of Zeisberger's History of the Bible; as, for instance, pages 119 and 120, third paragraph—*become confirmed* ; page, 123, second line from the bottom—*become universal*.   In these phrases I do not find *n'dellsin,* nor indeed any word to express *become;* which seems in the Delaware to be understood."

To these inquiries, Mr. Heckewelder replied in two different letters. In his first (in consequence of being requested to return an immediate answer) he merely gives a translation in Delaware of the English phrases proposed, without any comment or grammatical explanation, as follows :

" 1.   To become.
    Allumilissin—elsin.

2.   I was once bad, I have now become good.
    *Nemomachtschilissihump, schukmetschi n'nolilissi.**

3.   The man is become as one of us.
    Na lenno lüssu, elsiyenk.

4.   What will become of his dreams ?
    Ta hatsch léke eechdelungwamoaguna untschi? or, *koecu hatsch w'delungwamoagana untschi ?* what benefit will he derive from his dreams ? †

5.   What is become of him ?
    Ta eli achpit ? (where is he ?) or, *ta uchtenden ?* how is he ? what is he about ? or, *ta léke hockeyal,* how does it look about him ? (*Germ.* Wie sieht es um ihn aus ?)

6.   To them gave he power to become the sons of God.
    Milap nikik allewussowoagan wentschitsch gask wequi-semuxit na-Gettanittowit ; or, milap nekik wdallewussoagan wentschitschgaski getannellowitall quisemaouna."

Mr. Heckewelder's second letter (of Oct. 13) contains a minute consideration of the word *become,* with an explanation of the true import of the different words by which it is expressed in the Delaware language ; and the whole letter

---

* "*Machtschi,* bad ; *schuk,* but ; *metschi,* ready, already ; *olilis,* good, (from *wulit.*) P. S. D."

† " *Nane* léke*tsch ;* amen, so be it, so may it happen ; *koecu,* what, something. P. S. D."

is so interesting, and throws so much light upon the structure of the Indian languages, that I am unwilling to abridge it. He writes as follows :

" By your two letters of the 8th and 9th of October, I discover that my first answer to your questions had not reached you. In that I attempted to translate the Scripture passages quoted by you, for the purpose of discovering what word the Delawares have for our word BECOME, or TO BECOME ; the German word for it being *werden*.

" I have since also given the quotations from Scripture, contained in your *last* letters, due consideration, but cannot discover any kind of word in the Delaware language, that would answer *generally* to the English word *become*, or the German *werden ;* neither do I believe there is such a word in their language. Yet they are never at a loss to convey the sense or meaning of this word by means of syllables from two or more words joined together ; and, indeed, often the *termination* of a word is sufficient for that purpose. The word *állemi*, which implies something *progressing, advancing towards a close, going on*, &c., is with them joined (generally *prefixed*) to a word which is expressive of the object it is progressing *to :* Thus, allemiKEN (to ripen) contains the meaning of the two words, *állemi gischiken*, which, when separated, are lengthened out as here written ; *tepiken* (Zeisb. p. 37) being the general word for any thing that bears fruit or grain, *when or being ripe, full-grown*, &c. Again : the word *allemilek* implies a *prediction*, or any thing *expected, progressing towards* the point, or towards establishing the fact ; as for instance, when I say—metschi ALLEMILEK *endchen ndelloweneep*, it is the same as saying, *all that I had said* (or *foretold*) is now coming to pass.

" In this way the word *become* is, in a manner, interwoven in the words of their language ; and by examining the passages you quote from Zeisberger's Translation, it will be found so. As, in his History of the Bible, p. 119, third paragraph, for the English word *increase*, or, *that they increased*, he has the word *allemikenéwo*, from the word *allemi gischiken* (the termination *ewo* signifying *they*) that is, *they became more numerous*.* At pages 126—7, where you take the word *wtellitch* to express *become*, (which word, however, has

* " The word *gischiken* is also applicable to the birth of an infant—*found born*. J. H."

a different signification) Zeisberger says—*ahanhocqui gischigá-pannik;* which words imply *an additional* or *extraordinary increase,* which had taken place in Egypt, &c.; and for the words—*the king became apprehensive,* Zeisberger has—*wentschi Sakima nechasop* wtellitsch wsami m'chelhittin, woak allowiwunan*—which is—*therefore the King became fearful, that by means of this increase they might finally be too powerful for them:* Here *sop* answers for *jealous.*

"The passage *wtell*itsch Sokenapâlan, which you quote from page 136, line 9—*nil milápanil Allouchsowoagan wentschitsch undamemensichtit Getannittowittink* is translated from the German text, which reads thus : *Denen gab er macht kinder Gottes zu werden. John* i. 12. The words *kinder zu werden* (in English, *to become children*) are expressed in the Indian word *undamemensíchtit ;* in which the two last syllables *ichtit* express the words *to become ;* (Germ. werden;) so that the two last words, *undamemensichtit Getannittowitink,* taken together, clearly imply *to become children of God.*

"The next passage you quote, (from page 108, and which you find in Matth. xviii. 3,)

	Mattatsch	gluppiwéque,	woak	mattatsch	amemensuwiwéque,
(ENG.	*If not*	*you turn back,*	*and*	*if not*	*as children ye become,)*
(GERM.	*Wo nicht*	*ihr umkehret,*	*und*	*wo nicht als die kinder ihr werdet,)*	

is as clearly set forth in their language as in either of ours; the word *become* (Germ. werden) being incorporated in the last word, or expressed by the last syllables *wiweque.* The word *wentschi* for *therefore,* (in German, *darum,*) Zeisb. p. 17, with the *tsch* at the end of it, points or directs to something that is to take place in future ; it implies as much as to say in German —*damit es geschehen möge.* The *reason* for my going there is also expressed by them thus—*wentschitsch na ayane.*

"Thus there are many Indian words, which, though necessary in explaining a thing, do not effect it without an additional word. For example, the word *anenáwi* would be, in German, *endlich,* and in English, *at last, finally,* &c. Now, by adding the syllable *itsch* to it, so as to make it *anenáwitsch,* it directs you *forward,* to something that is yet *to take place,* which is generally set forth in the next following word or words; as *anenawitsch*

---

* "For *nechásin* and *nechasil ;* see Zeisb. p. 30. *Nechasop,* in the text, stands for *jealous, fearful,* &c. J. H."

knémeneen Ménachking, that is, in German, *endlich werden w* *doch Pittsburg sehen—finally,* or *at last, we shall see Pittsbur* or (as is properly meant) *arrive at Pittsburg ;* the last word i this Indian expression being their name for that place.   But may also say—*auwiéwi knementsch Ménachking, finally we sha see (or arrive at) Pittsburg."*

These observations of Mr. Heckewelder will be rendere still more useful to the student, by the following addition: explanations, which were communicated in a subsequent le ter to Mr. Du Ponceau.   Mr. H. says—

" The structure of the Indian languages is, as you observ truly wonderful........I once believed myself competent to unde stand every word they used ; and I can still plainly see th necessity of every syllable. in a word, by which to explai themselves properly.   Not being able, however, to answe your questions intelligibly, otherwise than by examples, se ting forth words and phrases, which will lead to the re quired solution, I shall adopt that method.

" Thus with regard to the syllable UND.   I begin with th word *unden,* Zeisb. p. 16.   This (says Z.) is *to take fron* which so far is correct ; for, if an Indian becomes possessed an article not seen with him before, he will be asked—" r GUNDEN ?* *where did you get it ? or how did you come by it ?"* fo the word *unden* of itself instructs us, that the article was o tained at *some* place, or came to hand through or from *son* source.   As, *Zeisberger,* p. 67—UNDENUMMEN, *to take it fron* or, more properly, *to have obtained it (es bekommen)*—WUNF ENASIK, *where* it is to be got *from* (Zeisb. p. 72) points to *certain* place where the article *was* obtained or *may be had.*

" When the syllable UND or WEND is *prefixed,* in a *spiritu* sense, it applies to *favours, gifts,* &c., not to things purchase or on which a price is set.   Thus WENDENUXOWOAGAN, *receptio admittance.   Zeisb.* 111.—UNDOOCHWENALL, he came for *the* sake.   *Zeisb.* 67.—" *Christ undoochwenep getemaxitschit"* i Christ came for the purpose of (saving or relieving) the poo or needy.   WENDaptonachga, *of,* or *from the word. Zeisb.* 9 —Christ *wundaptonalgun,* Christ (by or through his word *speaks unto us* (that is, we do not ourselves *hear* him speal yet what he says is *directed to us*) *from his place of abode*

---

* In this word *gunden,* and some others, Mr. Heckewelder seems (accordin to the practice of German writers) to use the letter *g* for *k ;* this latter bein the usual prefix to denote the second person.

UNDEN *Christink*, it proceedeth or cometh *from* him; UND-*amemensemichtit, through* or *by*.......*to become,* &c.

"I can go no further in explaining the syllable *und* (from *unden*) than to add, that when used in a *temporal* sense, it implies *to get* or *have gotten, procured* or *purchased* such a thing or article from the place or person at the time named. In a *spiritual* sense, it is applied to a thing *obtained* by free will or through *grace*—to be *admitted, received,* BE, or BECOME *a partaker,* &c. of, in, or to whatever one or the other of the connected words indicates.

"WENTSCHI is simply *therefore* (Germ. *darum, um desswillen.*)

"WENTSCHITSCH is *thereby* (Germ. *dadurch*) and directs to the future.

"We have no such words as *nentschi, kentschi,* in the language. The letter *w,* in *wentschi,* does not point to the third person, but is necessary to distinguish that word from UNTSCHI, *from, of,* (*Zeisb.* 16.) which, being a general word, is frequently either wholly or partly incorporated in other words; as, for instance : *Ta untschiey—where does it come from ? Nik lennowak wemi* utenink UNTSCHI*jeyü—those men are all come from the city.*

"NUNTSCHI*hilla uteney*—I came, with speed, from the city. *Kuntschihilla* uteney—are *you* come, with speed, *from the city* ? *Untschihilleu* uteney—he came, speedily, from the city or town. Kuntschihillahummo uteney—are *you all* come from the city or town ?"*

To these remarks should be added a brief explanation of the terminations *muxit* and *sichtit,* which occur in some of the preceding examples :

"In looking over your letter (says Mr. H.) after I had written this, I find that I had not sufficiently explained the terminations *muxit* and *sichtit.* Please to turn to Zeisberger's Spelling Book, page 104, for the word MACHELEMUXOWOAGAN, *honour ;* p. 82, for the word MACHELEMUXIT,† he that is honoured ; and p. 52, for MACHELENDAM, to honour, &c. NOW MACHELEMAU or MACHELEMÆ is, *honour him,* &c.; MACHELEMUX*ichtit,* may be *or* become *honoured.* Now it will be understood as ex-

---

* " The syllables *hilla* (taken from the word *schihilla,* quickly, speedily) added to the word *untschi,* make the compound *untschihilla,* and denote either *quick running* or *riding.* J. H."

† " It is all the same whether I write this word *muxsit* or *mucksit :* I have seen the word *maxen* (shoes) written *mocksen,* &c. J. H."

actly the same thing, whether I say WENTSCHI MACHELEMUX-*ichtitetsch*, or WENTSCH*itsch* MACHELEMUX*ichtit*, to become honoured. The same thing takes place in the word UND-AMEMEN-*sichtit;* the future, *to be made, become*, in the first words, is in the termination *ichtitetsch;* in the last, it is partly in the termination of the word *wentschitsch*, and partly in the termination of the second word *ichtit*."

I cannot omit adding here (from a letter of Mr. Du Ponceau) the following elucidation of the Indian method of expressing our verbs :

"We are now (says he) upon the word *become;* and Mr. Heckewelder has told us, that there is no proper word for it in the language of the Delawares, but yet that they are never at a loss for a method of conveying that idea. Let us see how they go about it. Mr. H. instances the words *to become honoured;* in Delaware *wentschi machelemuxichtitetsch,* or (what is equivalent) *wentschitsch machelemuxichtit.* This may be parsed as follows :

"*Wentschi* (as explained in Mr. Heckewelder's letter) is *therefore; wentschitch* is *thereby,* and directs to the future.

"*Machelemuxichtit.* In the *Transactions of the Historical and Literary Committee,* (p. 445 of Mr. Heckewelder's Correspondence,) we have the substantive *machelemuxowoagan,* honour, or *the being honoured.* The verb is *machelendam* (3d conjug.) *to honour; machelemuxit* (particip.) *he who is honoured; machelemuxichtit* (3d pers. plur. conditional, or conjunctive) *if,* or *when they are honoured.* Observe, that the phrase *to be honoured* is here taken in a plural sense—*wentschimachelemuxichtitetsch* or *wentschitsch machelemuxichtit.* Tsch is the sign of the *future;* and it is a matter of indifference, says Mr. Heckewelder, whether it is suffixed to the preposition *by it,* or to the verb *to be honoured;* hence, the two modes of rendering the sentence. Thus "to become the children of God" is expressed in Zeisberger's Harmony, by " *wentschitsch undamemensichtit Getannittowitink;*" WENTSCHITSCH, *thereby in future,* UNDAMEMENSICHTIT, (from *awemens,* child,) *to become the children.* Here the word *become* is not at all used, but a compound verb, from the substantive *child,* expresses the idea ; as in the Latin word *beatificari* (a word formed much after the Indian manner) the syllable *fi* awakening in the mind the idea of *fieri;* but as there is no such word as *fieri* in the Indian (in the mere abstract sense) the same idea is differently expressed. Lastly : GETANNITTOWITINK, *of God—ink* or *onk* is a termination of *relation*, and here expresses the genitive. See *Zeisberger's* Grammar : " Nihillalquonk Allogewoaganall, *God's the Lord's works.*"

The preceding discussion respecting the verbs *to be* and *to become*, has been confined (as the reader will have observed) to two of the Indian languages only, the Delaware of the present day, and the Massachusetts as spoken a century and a half ago. But since the correspondence of Mr. Heckewelder and Mr. Du Ponceau, I have been enabled to extend my inquiries on the present question to some other Indian dialects; though not with the same minuteness and certainty as in the case of the Delaware language. For the information which I have obtained, I am indebted to the Rev. Herman Daggett, Superintendant of the *Foreign Missionary School*, established at Cornwall, in the State of Connecticut ; who, notwithstanding the pressure of ill health, was so obliging as to make particular inquiries for me on this subject of the different Indian pupils under his care. In his letter to me, of the 22d of October, 1821, he says——

." I have, strictly speaking, but *four* Indian languages in my school ; the Choctaw, the Cherokee, the Muhhekunneau (or Stockbridge) and the Iroquois, including the Oneida, Tuscarora and Caughnewaga. The youth of these nations, or tribes, agree in saying, as far as I can make them understand the subject, that *they have no substantive verb*. Where we should say, *I am here*, they can only say, *I here*, or *I stand* or *live here*. I have now but one *Stockbridge* lad ; he recognizes, in some measure, his own language in the few words you have given from *Eliot*, but appears to know nothing of the verb conjugated by *Cotton*.* The word *nuttinniin*, he says, signifies *always the same, without change ;* and *nutapip*, *I was born*, or *I born*.

" The attempts of the different youths at translating the given passages [of scripture] are not very satisfactory. Some of them have a word, or part of a word, which, they say, signifies AM or WAS, in *connexion ;* but they say it has not that meaning *by itself.* Their translation, they say, is good Cherokee or good Choctaw, &c.; but when I try to bring them to

---

* The words of *Eliot* here alluded to, were—Negonne *onk Abrahamwi nutapip*—John viii. 58 ; and the verb conjugated by *Cotton* was ainneat, which is given above, at p. xxv. As to the close affinity between the *Muhheakunneau* (Mohegan) and the Massachusetts, see above, *Introductory Observations*, p. 19.

explain and analyze, they are at a loss......I can plainly discover that there is a beautiful contexture in their languages."*

From the whole of this investigation, then, it appears—

1. That the observation made by Eliot, at the very early period when he wrote, that there was " no complete distinct word for the verb substantive" in the Massachusetts language, is very fully confirmed by what we find to be the case in the *Delaware* language ; which is the main stock of the Massachusetts and other northern dialects, and from which we may reason (in respect to general properties) to the derivative dialects, without much hazard of falling into any material errours.

2. That the Massachusetts verb *nuttinniin* (or *n'tinniin*, as it would now be written) which Eliot sometimes uses for our verb *to be*, and sometimes for *become*, is nothing more than an *approximation* to the strict meaning of those English words.

But the precise import of the Massachusetts verb *nuttinniin* does not yet appear so clearly as to leave no uncertainty upon the subject ; though it seems to have a close affinity with the Delaware verb *n'dellsin*, and probably is (as Mr. Du Ponceau has above observed) the very corresponding verb in that kindred dialect. If, upon further investigation, this should prove to be the fact, beyond all doubt, then we shall need no other authority for the fundamental idea of this verb, than that of Mr. Heckewelder, who informs us, that in the *Delaware* it is, *I act so, I act for myself* (in German, *so bin ich gestellt.*) Yet, until the identity of the two verbs is incontrovertibly established, it may be allowable in an inquiry of this nature to offer even conjectures ; with the hope, that if such conjectures should not be entirely well founded in themselves, they may be the means of exciting such further investigations, as may at last conduct us to the true solution of the problem. Under this impression, I shall submit one other view of the subject, which has occurred to me upon a fresh examination of Eliot's Grammar, and some other works relative to the dialects of our northern Indians. I offer it as a mere conjecture ; and I should not venture to do even that, if I had not obtained the approbation of Mr. Du Ponceau himself, who thinks this view not unworthy of being submitted to the reader.

Eliot, in p. 23 of his Grammar, has the following curious remark : " There be also suppletive syllables of no significa-

* For specimens of the *Cherokee* language, the reader is referred to Dr. Jarvis's *Discourse on the Religion of the Indian Tribes of North America ;* the learned Notes of which contain much valuable information on the *Languages* of the Indians.

tion but for ornament of the word, as *tit, tin, tinne ;* and these, in way of an elegancy, receive the *affix,* which belongeth to the noun or verb following, as *nuttit, kuttit, wuttit,* NUTTIN, *kuttin, wuttin,* NUTTINNE, *kuttinne, wuttinne.*"

During a very recent perusal of his Grammar, this remark attracted my notice ; and it immediately occurred to me that, possibly, the suppletive syllable *tinne* might be a constituent part of the verb *nuttinniin ;* in which case the verb itself would be simply *nuttiin,* or (as we should now write it) *n'tiin.* Pursuing the investigation, upon this hypothesis, I found in *Cotton's* MS. Vocabulary several instances, in which the suppletive *tin* (as well as some of the other suppletives) appeared to be thus incorporated into different verbs with the affixes of the different persons, in conformity with Eliot's observation. This led me to continue my inquiries for a verb of the form I have mentioned (*n'tiin*) *;* and I had the satisfaction at last of meeting with it in *Roger Williams's Vocabulary* of the *Naraganset* dialect ; which is now well known to be nearly the same language with the *Massachusetts.* In that Vocabulary, the verb in question occurs in the three following phrases ; in one of which, however, it is somewhat obscured by the author's very irregular orthography :

" Yo ntfin . . . . I *live* here.
Tou wuttfin ? . . . . where *lives* he ?
Tuckuttiin [tou kuttfin ?] . . . . where *keep* you ?"*

Now, if *Eliot's* verb *nuttinniin* is in fact the same with *Williams's* verb *n'tiin,* the signification of it, as the reader perceives, is very different from that of the pure substantive verb ; some other idea being united with that of mere existence in the abstract. How far this analysis of the verb *nuttinniin* may be well founded, is submitted to the candid reader, with all that hesitation, which ought to be felt by one, who has no more knowledge of the Indian languages than I possess.

Thus far the present remarks have been directed to the meaning of Eliot's verb *nuttinniin ;* and it now only remains, to ascertain the signification of his other substitutes for the

---

* The English word *keep* seems to be here used by Williams, in the provincial signification, which it has in some parts of New England at the present day ; that is, in the sense of *to stay, reside,* or (as Williams says in the other two phrases) *to live.* See his *Key,* chap. i. in *Massachusetts Historical Collections,* vol. v. pp. 80, 81.

" complete substantive verb," which occur in the texts above cited (p. xxxi.) The explanations of these last will take up the less time, as the remarks upon the former, in connexion with the general question, have been extended to so great a length. I shall give them in a very concise form, as they occur in Mr. Du Ponceau's letters to me. He says—

"I have studied the problems, and think I have gone a great way towards solving them.

"I. Rev. i. 4. From him which is, and which was, and which is to come—*Wutch noh, noh koh, noh koh mô, noh paont.*

Wutch (Delaw. *wentschi*) from.

Noh, *ke, him* (Gram. p. 7.) used again for *who* or *which.*

Koh. This word is embarrassing, because of the letter *k*, indicating the second person. I am unable at present to explain it in a manner perfectly satisfactory to myself.

Noh paont. This is easily explained from the Delaware. In that language, we find pahump, *to come;* peu, *he comes;* pewak, *they come.* Paont is undoubtedly an inflexion of the same verb. In Eliot's Grammar, p. 22, we find woi napeh-nont, *O! that it were;* which literally is—*O that it came* (*to pass.*)

Mo. That mo is a particle indicative of the past, I have little doubt; as in Gen. xxxi. 40, above quoted : yeu mo nuttinnahin—yeu, *this,* (used for *thus*)—mo, *heretofore,* nuttin-nahin, *was so or so* (from *n'dellsin,*) as stated in the notes before communicated.

"If I am right thus far, then every thing is explained but *koh,* which I cannot yet sufficiently account for.

"II. Rev. xvii. 8...........and yet is—*kah noh yeuyeu* apit.

Kah noh yeuyeu apit—and he, this this (yeu yeu, *Gram.* p. 8.) *is there; ápit* (pronounced as *épit* in German) *illic stat. Yeu* duplicated, perhaps used for *which.*

"III. Gen. v. 4...........*kah matta na* wutapein.

Na is an expletive which I cannot explain.

Wutapein (Delaw. *w'dappin,* he is there.) See *Zeisb. Delaware Grammar.*

"IV. Psalm xxxvii. 36...........matta *ohtano,* was not.

Ohtano is probably a form of the same verb, and means he was not there. *W'dano, w'tano, ohtano;* the *o, u* and *oh* are often used by Eliot for the Delaware *w* sibilant. For the same reason, we say, the *Ottawas, Utawas,* while their proper name is *W'tawas,* or *Wtawas,*"

II. Numerals.

Eliot, in his Grammar, gives as the numeral *one*, the word *nequt* only, corresponding to the Delaware *n'gutti*, and the Naraganset *nquit*. But in his Bible he uses also the word *pasuk*, corresponding to the Abnaki *pézekou* of Father Râle's dictionary, and the Naraganset *pâwsuck* of Roger Williams's Key. Now, in reading Cotton's valuable Vocabulary, the following curious distinction, in the use of these two different numerals, attracted my notice:

> " *Nequt*, a thing that is past.
> *Pasuk*, a thing in being."

I lost no time in communicating this distinction of Cotton's to Mr. Du Ponceau, with a wish that he would ascertain from Mr. Heckewelder, whether any thing of the kind was to be found in the *Delaware* language. This circumstance gave rise to the following interesting observations on the Delaware *numerals*:

" The Delawares (says Mr. H. in his first letter) have the following words for *one*, viz: *n'gutti*, *máwat*, *mauchsu* and *majouchsu*. The two first are generally made use of for what is *inanimate*; the latter two, for what is *animate*. *Páschuk* is the true Mahicanni word for *one*."

In a subsequent letter, Mr. H. gives the following more copious explanation in respect to the *Delaware* numerals; which serves at the same time to elucidate the curious structure of the Indian languages:

" Not being quite satisfied with the partial answer I gave you in a hurry respecting the numeral *one*, I will now expatiate more fully thereon; first, pointing out what words the Delawares have in their language, equally necessary to be known, in addition to the one above quoted; as much depends, in speaking their language, upon having each word in its proper place; for although the numeral *n'gutti*, for *one*, may be in a manner considered as the *general* word in this language for the number *one*, (be the same *animate* or *inanimate*) yet it is not always the case. Indeed the *first* syllable of that word, *n'gut*, (*I* leave out always the prefixed *n*, there being no necessity for it, as it is only put there to explain the numeral; as by saying " *one single one*") I say, that al-

though this first syllable is very useful, and *prefixed* to a grea
number of *compound* words, all which tend to show that this
syllable *gut* cannot be dispensed with, as will by and by be
shown by examples; yet, the *latter* syllable of the numeral
the *ti*, is not only in numerous cases useless, but would be
even improper, if retained.   *Ex.* The Indian name or word
for a *one-legged* person, being *gut-gat*, is a compound of two
words; *gut*, from GUTTI, *one*, and *gát*, from WICHGAT, *the leg*,
GUTGATSU, *he is one-legged*, or *has but one leg*.   GUTOKENAK is
the word for *one day*; GUTAWICAN, *one fathom* (*awícan* being the word for *one fathom*, or six feet;) GUT-TAPACHKI, *one
hundred*, &c.   Generally speaking, the Indians are very nice
in the selecting of words.   I will give you such as are in conjunction with the one in question, viz. GUTTI, *one* : *Zeisb*. 11,
' MAWAT (only) *one*.'   *Zeisb*. 13, MAYAAT (is the same in the
Minsey.)   The two latter of these three words can *in no wise*
be made use of with that which is *animate* ; on the other hand,
the words MAUCHSU and MAYAUCHSU are the proper words
for what is animate : MAUCHSU LENNO is *one man* ; MAUCHSU
TIPAS, *one* (single) *fowl*, &c. (*Mayauchsu* is the Minsey word
for the same. *See Zeisberger*, 52, *at bottom*.)   If I meant
to say to a *Lenape*, that *of all the men* who had returned
from hunting, only *one* (single person) had killed a deer, I
could not make use of the numeral *n'gutti*, for that *one*, but
I must say—*bischi apallauwiwak lennowelk weemi, allod máuchsu*
(or *mayauchsu*) *schuk, mescheu*.   See, for mayauchsu, *Zeisb*.
p. 52, *at bottom* ; and for MEmayauchsiyENK, *every* ONE *of us*,
MEmayauchsiyEEK, *every* ONE *of you*, *Zeisb*. p. 105.

  " You inquire further, whether it is the same in the Delaware, as *Cotton* says it is in the *Natick* [Massachusetts] that
there are ' two words for the numeral *one*—*n'gutte* or *nequt*,
for a thing *past*, and *pasuk*, for a thing present.'   In this
remark, I consider *Cotton* to be under a mistake; for *I am
sure*, that the *Mahicanni* word *n'gutte* (the same as the Delaware *n'gutti* or *gutti*) is a *general* word, and in constant use
for the *present*.   The Mahicanni say—*guttē* or *gutta* for *one* :
" *Gutta-gún* (in Delaware, *gutti-gull*) ONE *six-penny piece*—
n'guttóxena (Delaw. *guttáxen*) ONE *pair of shoes*, &c.   I presume the Natick word *nequt* answers to the Delaware *gut-
TEN*, since it points to the *past*, as for instance—*gútTEN
n'gachti angeln*, ONCE *I was on the point of dying* ; *gutTEN woa-
pan*, ONCE *of a morning* ; *schuk gutTEN* Cuequenáku *m'pahn*,
ONLY ONCE *I have been at Philadelphia*, &c.   The Delawares
have also the word *nekti* (*See Zeisb*. p. 14) much in use

when speaking of any *one* thing or article, and not being possessed of more than the one of that kind.

" I have already said (in my last letter) that *paschuk* is a true *Mahicanni* word for *one ;* and so I suppose *nequt* to be, in its proper place.

" You inquire how this word *paschuk* is pronounced, whether as in German, or as in English, with the acute *a*. I always write words according to the pronunciation of the Germans ; but in writing the word according to the English alphabet, I should write it *pawshuk*.

" I will add one observation on certain differences between the languages of the *Mohegans* (or Mahicanni) and the *Delawares*, both in respect to the words themselves, and the manner of pronouncing. The Mohegans, by *changing* some of their letters in words from that of the Delawares, by *dropping* others entirely, and by drawing out their words in speaking, give the language a different sound from what it otherwise would have, were they to abide by the proper letters, and speak *off hand* as the Delawares do. They generally drop the letter L of the Delawares, and supply its place with the letter N ; and where the Delawares have a *single* vowel, they sound their word as if there were *two*. For example :

For the Delaware	. .	*korcu*	(what) they say,	GAQUAI ;
For	. . . .	*auween*	(who)	. . . . .	AWAAN ;
For	. . . .	*ni*	(I)	. . . .	NIA ;
For	. . . .	*oyos*	(meal)	. . . . .	WIAAS ;
For	. . . .	*niluna*	(we)	. . . . . .	NIANA ;
For	. . . .	*dee*	(heart)	. . . . .	OTTAHA, &c.

To these remarks on the Indian *numerals*, it may be useful to add an important observation made by Mr. Heckewelder, in the *Transactions of the Historical and Literary Committee*. He there says—" On the subject of the numerals, I have had occasion to observe, that they sometimes differ very much in languages derived from the same stock. Even the *Minsi*, a tribe of the Lenape or Delaware nation, have not all their numerals like those of the *Unami* tribe, which is the principal among them."*

* Correspondence with Mr. Du Ponceau, in the *Transactions*, p. 381.

INDEX OF INDIAN WORDS IN ELIOT'S GRAMMAR; INCLUDING SELECT WORDS FROM HIS TRANSLATION OF THE BIBLE.

Advertisement. THE following Index was originally intended by the editor to include only those Indian words, which are contained in Eliot's *Grammar;* and Mr. Du Ponceau had prepared (from the *Grammar* and *Bible* together) a separate List of words, corresponding to the seventy English words of the *Comparative Vocabularies* in Dr. Barton's *New Views of the Tribes and Nations of America.* But, as many of the words in Mr. Du Ponceau's List were also to be found in the *Grammar,* and would of course be repeated in an index to that work, the editor has (with the concurrence of Mr. Du Ponceau) incorporated the whole into the present Index. In order however, to enable the reader to select from it all the words, which correspond to those of Dr. Barton's List, and thus supply the want of a separate Vocabulary, such corresponding words are here printed in SMALL CAPITALS. The words selected from the *Bible,* by Mr. Du Ponceau, will be readily distinguished by their having no references to pages annexed to them.

A.

Page

A (a vowel often inserted for the sake of euphony)   *See* Gram. p. 9

Ahque (*adv. of forbidding*) beware, do not 21

ACHQUNNON, rain. *See* SOKANON

Ah (an inflexion of *animate* nouns.) *See* Gram. . . 8

Ahquompak, when . . . 21

Ahtuk, a deer 9

Alúm (*in the Nipmuk dialect*) a dog 2

ANOGQS, a star 9

Anomut, within 21

Anue (*adv. of choosing*) more rather; . . . . . 21 also *a sign of the comparative degree:* Anue menuhkesu, more strong 15

Anúm, a dog 2

Ao, oco *and* yeuco; *terminations added to nouns, adjectives, adverbs, &c. in order to change them into verbs substantive;* as, wosketomp, *a man,* wosketompoco, *he is a man, or he be-*

came *a man;* wompi, *white,* wompiyeuco, *it is white,* 12, 1

Arúm (*in the* "Northern" *dialect*) a dog . . . . .

As; *a syllable added to the indicative mode of verbs, in order to make it interrogative. See* Gram. p. 27. *It is also used, to change the present tense into the preterite. See* Gram. pp. 62,6

Ash (*adv. of continuation*) still 2

Ash (the *plural* termination of *inanimate* nouns.) *See* Gram. 1

ASKONUH, skin

Askook, a snake *or* worm .

Asquam (*adv. of choosing*) not yet 2

Assootu, foolish 1

Asuh, or 2

At; *a termination used in forming the infinitive mode, which is done by adding this termination to the indicative, and taking away the suffix* 2

At, en; in, ut: (*prep.*) in, at
  or to 22
Ayim, he made 8

C.

Chaubohkish; *except, besides* 22
Chuh (*adv. of calling; the
  same as* hóh) 21

E.

E (*used as the termination of
  the inanimate form of some
  adjectives.*) See Gram. p. 13
E *or* u; *the common terminations of adverbs; as* wame
  or wamu, *all;* menuhke *or*
  menuhku, *strongly* . . 21
Ehhoh, hah (*adv. of exhorting
  or encouraging*) . . . 21
Ehoh, (*interj. of encouraging*) 22
En. *See* át
Emes *or* es; *terminations
  added to primitive nouns
  to make them diminutives;*
  emes *is the least of them* 12
Es (mark of *diminutive.* See
  emes)
Es *and* esu (*terminations of
  the animate form of some
  adjectives.*) See Gram. p. 13
Eum, oom, *or* um; *the sign of
  the "possessive rank" of
  nouns* 12

H.

Hah; *the same as* ehoh . . 22
Hó (*interj. of wondering*) 22
Hoo, body
Hóh (*adv. of calling; the
  same as* chuh) 21
Hoo; *the same as* hó . . . 22
Horsemes; *diminutive of the
  English word* horse . . 12
Horsesog; *the plural of the
  English word* horse . . 12
Howan, who 7
Howanig; *plural of* howan 7
19

Hussun, a stone 10
Hussunemes; *diminutive of*
  hussun 12

I.

I (*used as the termination of
  the inanimate form of some
  adjectives.*) See Gram. p. 13
In (*prep.*) See át
Ishkont, lest 22

K.

Keek, thy house 11
Keekit, in thy house . . . 11
Keekou, your house (*plur.*) 11
Keekuwout, in your house (*pl.*) 11
Ken, thou 7
Kenaau, ye 7
Kenawun *or* neenawun, we 7
Kenuppoowonuk, he died for
  thee* 18
Kenuppoowonukqun, he died
  for us* 18
Kenuppoowonukoo, he died for
  you,* 18
Kenutcheg, thy hand . . . 11
Kenutcheganash *or* kenutche-
  gash, thy hands . . . 11
Kenutcheganoo, your hand (*pl.*) 11
Kenutchegash. *See* kenut-
  cheganash
Kenutcheganoowout,
  your hands 11
Kesuk, heaven
Kesukod, day
Kesukquieu, toward heaven 21
Koon, snow
Koowadchansh, I keep thee 17
Koowadchanumoush, I keep it
  for thee *or* for thy use . 17
Koowadchanumwanshun, I
  keep it for thee, I act in
  thy stead* 18

* "This form [of the verb] is of
great use in Theologie, to express
what Christ hath done for us."
          Gram. p. 18.

---

* " Mâssa-chusett- an hill in the form of an Arrow's Head." Cotton's MS. Vocabulary of the Language of the Plymouth Indians.

° " When the action is doubled or frequented, &c. this notion hath not a distinct form, but is expressed by doubling the first syllable of the word." Gram. p. 17.

---

* See Mr. Du Ponceau's remarks on these two forms of the plural, p. xix. of his Notes.

† Cotton, in his MS. Vocabulary of the Language of the Plymouth In-

dians, has this remark—" Nequt, a thing that is past : Pasuk, a thing in being." But see the observations on this subject, p. xlv. of the preceding Notes.

N'puhkuk, my head.   *See*
PUHKUK
Nuhog, my body.   *See* hog
NUKON, night
Nummissis, my sister
NUNKOMP, a young man, a
youth   9
Nunkompaemes (*diminutive
of* nunkomp)   12
Nunkompaes (*diminutive of*
nunkomp) 12
NUNKSQAU,* a girl . . .   9
Nunksquaemes (*diminutive
of* nunksquau) . . .   12
Nunksquaes (*diminutive of*
nunksquau)   12
NUNNAUMON, my son
Nunnogkus, my belly.   *See*
nogkus
Nunnuppꝏwonuk, he died for
me   18
Nunnutcheg, my hand . .   11
Nunnutcheganash, my hands   11
Nunnutcheganum, our hand   11
Nunnutchegannunnonut, our
hands   11
NUPPꝏNK, death
Nuskon, my bone.   *See* uskon
Nusseet, my foot.   *See* seet
Nutcheg.   *See* menutcheg
Nuttah, my heart.   *See* metah
and tah   11
Nuttahhun, our heart.   *See*
metah *and* tah   11
Nuttaunoh, my daughter.   *See*
taunoh
Nuttin.   *See* tin   23
Nuttꝏn, my mouth
Nux ; yea, yes   21

---

* The last syllable of this word is
printed in the original edition of the
Grammar as it is in the present one
(*qau*) ; but the diminutive, at p. 12,
has the same syllable printed *qua*, as
it is also in the Bible.   See *Joel* iii.
3 ; *Zech.* viii. 5.   The form *qau*,
therefore, seems to be an errour of
the press.

Nuxyeuꝏutch, let it be yea.
James v. 12   16

O.

Og (the *plural* termination of
animate nouns.)
See Gram. p. 9
Oh (*an inflexion* of *animate
nouns.*)   *See* Grammar, p. 8
OKASOH, mother
OHKE, earth
Ohkeiyeu (*adv.*) towards the
earth   21
Ongash *and* onganash (*the
plural termination of ver-
bal nouns in* ONK.)
See Gram. p. 10
Onk ; *a termination often
added to verbs*, in order to
turn them into nouns   13, 20
Onkoue, beyond   21
Oꝏ.   *See* aꝏ
ꝏm.   *See* cum
ꝏsqheonk, blood
ꝏwee (*interj. of sorrow*) .   22
Oxemes (*diminutive of the
English word*) ox   .   9
Oxesog (*plur. of the English
word* ox) oxen   9

P.

Pа ; *a particle added to the
indicative mode, to give it
the sense of the first person of the imperative* .   25
Pagwodche (*adv. of doubting*)
it may be   22
Pasuk (*numeral*) one.   *See
the note on* nequt
Paswu, lately   21
Paummuonat, to pay* . .   42

---

* Roger Williams says, this is "a
word newly made from the English

Paummauóunat, not to pay . 58

Peasik or peesik, small ; *used in expressing a degree of comparison* 15

PETUHQUNNEG, bread

Pigsemes (*diminutive of the English word*) pig . . 12

Pish. *See* mos

POMANTAMÓONK, life

POPON, winter

PSUKSES, a little bird . . 12

Puppinashim, a beast . . 0

PUHKUK, a head

Q.

Quah (*interj. of disdaining*) 22

Qunnuhtug (*from qunni, long, and* mehtug, *wood or tree*) *used to denote a* pike . . 15

Qussuk, a rock 10

Qut, but 22

S.

Sasabbath-dayeu, every sabbath (*made a frequentative by doubling the first syllable. See note on the word* mohmoeg.)

Saup, tomorrow 21

SEPU, river

SEET, foot

Sheepsemes (*diminutive of the English word*) sheep 12

Sohsúmóonk, forest

SOKANON, SOKANUNK ; rain

Sun, sunnummatta? (*adv. of asking*) is it, or is it not? 21

---

word *pay.*" *Key into the Languages of America,* ch. xxv. ; in *Mass. Hist. Collect.* vol. v. p. 100. Williams writes the first person singular, indicative mode, *cuppáimish,* I will pay you ; but Eliot writes it *kuppaumush,* at the same time directing the reader to pronounce *pay* and not *pau.* See *Gram.* p. 28.

T.

TAH, the heart. *See* metah

Tahshé ; *a suppletive word used with the numerals.* See *Gram.* 14

TASKON, horn

TAUNOH, daughter

Teanuk, presently . . . 21

Teaogkn (*adv.*) rather, unfinished 21

Tiadche, unexpectedly . . 22

Tin, tinne, tit ; *suppletive syllables used "for ornament of the word." See* Gram. 23

Tinne. *See* tin

Tit. *See* tin

Toh ; *annexed to every person and variation in the optative mood.* See p. 65. *See also* nahpenont

Toh (*adverb of doubting*) it may be 22

TOHKOI, it was cold

Tohkónogque, although . . 22

Tohneit, if 22

Tohsu ; *a suppletive, used with the numerals* . . 14

Tohsunash, how many . . 8

Tohsuog, how many . . . 8

Tohwutch, why 20

TOOHPU ; ice, frost

TOON, mouth. *See* muttoon

Tummunk, the beaver . . 9

U.

Uh (an inflexion of *animate* nouns.) *See* Grammar, p. 8

Um. *See* cum

Us ; *a syllable added to the present tense in order to form the preterite* . 62, 63

USKON, a bone

Ut. *See* ût

Uttiyeu, or tanyeu (*pron. rel.*) which 7

Uttiyeu (*adv.*) where . . 21

POSTSCRIPT.

THE following Extract of a letter from Mr. Du Ponceau was to have been added to the Notes on Eliot's Grammar, as published in the *Historical Collections*; but an accidental delay rendered this impracticable. The importance of it, however, has induced the Editor to add it to those copies of the Grammar, which are printed in a separate pamphlet.

Extract of a Letter from Mr. Du Ponceau to the Editor.

" In Barton's *New Views* (*Appendix*, p. 5) there is a pretended List of the *numerals* of the *Nanticoke* language, which Dr. Barton says he obtained from Mr. *Pyrlæus*, through Mr. Heckewelder, and which was found among the papers of the former. After I had for some time begun the study of the Indian languages, it struck me, that these numerals could not be those of the *Nanticoke*, of which I had a vocabulary, shewing it to be an idiom nearly allied to the Delaware. I therefore took the first opportunity of asking information of Mr. Heckewelder; and the result of what he told me is contained in the following Note, which I made at the time in my copy of Dr. Barton's work :

'April 30, 1818. Mr. Heckewelder told me this day, that the Nanticoke language is a dialect of the Algonkin or Delaware; and so it appears by the vocabularies communicated by him to Mr. Jefferson. He may have formerly believed otherwise, and may have told Dr. Barton what he states above. The above list of numerals was indeed made by Mr. Pyrlæus and found among his papers; but it does not appear to what language it belongs.'

" I had lost sight of those numerals and my note, when Mr. ————————— told me some days ago, that he had discovered a curious fact, which was, that the numerals of the *Nanticoke* were exactly similar to those of the *Bambara Negroes*. I asked him, whether he alluded to Dr. Barton's *Nanticoke* numerals; and upon his answering in the affirmative, I informed him that those were not genuine; and we both came to the conclusion, that either Mr. Pyrlæus himself, before he came to this country, had been a Moravian missionary in Africa, or that he had obtained the numerals from some of his brethren who had been; or, perhaps, that he had taken them from some Negro in this country. But it is not the less true, that if the same observation should occur to an European, he might be incautiously led to the conclusion, that the American languages were nearly connected with those of the Negroes of Africa; then the inference would be drawn, that the American race was evidently derived from the African, theories would arise without end, and ingenious arguments would be found, *a priori*, to prove the migration of the *Africans* to this Continent; and even the physical causes would be discovered, which turned their black colour into red, and the wool of their heads into hair. It is right, that the learned should be put on their guard against errours of this kind. I subjoin the different numerals here referred to:

	" *True Nanticoke Numerals.**	*Dr. Barton's supposed Nanticoke Numerals.*	*Numerals of the Bambara Africans.†*
" One	Nickquit	Killi	Killi
Two	Na-eez	Filli	Foolla
Three	Kis-whu	Sábo	Sabba
Four	Yaugh-whu	Náno	Nani
Five	Nup-pai-a	Túro	Looroo
Six	Hoquuttah	Wóro	Wora
Seven	My-yay-wah	Wóllango	Worroola
Eight	Tzah	Sécki	Sagi
Nine	Pasa-conque	Cóllengo	Konunto
Ten	Millah	Tà	Ta. "

* "This list was obtained from a vocabulary taken in the year 1792, by Gen. William Vans Murray, at a *Nanticoke* Indian town in Dorset County Maryland, and communicated by him to Mr. Jefferson, who gave it to me. Compare this list with the *Delaware* numerals in Historical Transactions pp. 374, 375.   P. S. D."

† " From Bowditch's Mission to Ashantee, p. 193, Appendix.   See the same work for the numerals of the true *Mandingo*, and also of a corrupt *Bambara* or Mandingo dialect.   *Ibid. and p.* 182.   P. S. D."

Corrections in Eliot's Grammar.

1. INTROD. OBSERVAT. p. 233, line 30, *after the word* America, *insert* on the East side of the Mississippi.
   Ibid. p. 234. The MS. copy of Eliot's Grammar, here mentioned, was presented by the American Philosophical Society, on the motion of Mr. Du Ponceau.
   Ibid. p. 235, lines 14, 15, *dele* the aid of.
2. In the GRAM. p. 66, line 20, *for* deficile *read* difficile.
3. In the NOTES,
   p. vi. line 29, *for* Chatimachas *read* Chetimachas.
   p. vii. line 17, *after* Etchemins *insert* or Abenakis.
   p. x. line 26, *for* cortesario *read* cortesano.
   p. xiii. line 10, *for* always uni co *read* almost always mute.
   p. xiv. line 11, *after* Ibid. 13. *insert* Wuthassuneutunk wuttanoh Zion " The wall of the daughter of Zion."   *Lamentat.* ii. 8.
   p. xxxii. (in the note at bottom) *for* xxxv. *read* xxv.

THE END.

Printed in the United States
58641LVS00004B/39

9 781419 177569